English Now

5

Rob Francis

Illustrated by Jan Wade

NELSON
CENGAGE Learning™

Australia • Brazil • Japan • Korea • Mexico • Singapore • Spain • United Kingdom • United States

English Now 5

Text: Rob Francis
Illustrations: Jan Wade

English Now

Text © 2003 Rob Francis
Illustrations © 2003 Jan Wade

Copyright Notice
This Work is copyright. No part of this Work may be reproduced, stored in a retrieval system, or transmitted in any form or by any means without prior written permission of the Publisher. Except as permitted under the *Copyright Act 1968*, for example any fair dealing for the purposes of private study, research, criticism or review, subject to certain limitations. These limitations include: Restricting the copying to a maximum of one chapter or 10% of this book, whichever is greater; Providing an appropriate notice and warning with the copies of the Work disseminated; Taking all reasonable steps to limit access to these copies to people authorised to receive these copies; Ensuring you hold the appropriate Licences issued by the Copyright Agency Limited ("CAL"), supply a remuneration notice to CAL and pay any required fees.

ISBN 978 0 17 011633 6

Cengage Learning Australia
Level 7, 80 Dorcas Street
South Melbourne, Victoria Australia 3205
Phone: 1300 790 853

Cengage Learning New Zealand
Unit 4B Rosedale Office Park
331 Rosedale Road, Albany, North Shore NZ 0632
Phone: 0800 449 725

For learning solutions, visit **cengage.com.au**

Printed in China by RR Donnelley Asia Printing Solutions Limited
8 9 10 11 12 13 14 16 15 14 13 12

For the teacher

English Now Book 5 is the sixth in a series of seven activity books designed to implement the new English Syllabus in schools. Activities are developed from concepts, strategies and skills outlined in the new English curriculum.

Pointers for Levels 3, 4 and 5 are provided for each activity within each unit in the book. Teachers can obtain a clear picture of the level/s achieved by each student.

Sixteen units in the book cover a wide variety of school-based topics that are appropriate for the development and experiences of students in Year 5. The teacher should develop and encourage reading, writing, talking, listening, spelling and grammar by building upon the child's existing knowledge and experiences.

The purpose of the book is to assist the teacher. Intense teacher input is required and the book will serve as a written record of student performance and achievement in the learning of English.

It is up to the teacher's judgement as to how the units are treated. For example, the teacher may teach two units, focus on and address a writing tutorial and set another unit for homework. However, it is recommended that three units and a writing tutorial be taught each term.

Pointers and Levels give flexibility to the program. It allows students to not only work at their level, but also to strive to achieve pointers in the next level.

Where necessary, lessons begin with a clear statement of task. Teachers and parents should ask the child to read the instructions carefully, but where necessary, read the instructions to children and discuss the activity so it is understood.

When used correctly, this book will develop in students a positive attitude and greater confidence in Talking and Listening, Reading, Writing, Spelling and Grammar.

Developing competence in English is a process that depends on a child doing, experiencing and sharing. **English Now** is a resource that assists learning in a fun way, while ensuring concepts are taught and some experience recorded at the child's level of development.

Message to Parents

School provides learning experiences and develops skills, but the home is also vital to the child's educational progress.

Learning is a developmental process that begins at birth and continues throughout life, and parents play a vital role in their child's learning. This series of books encourages parents to help their child to broaden experiences, participate in the reading process and develop competence in English.

Research has shown that parents and teachers working together make learning easier for the child. As you encourage and praise your child's work, understanding of the English language will develop. Help, praise and encouragement at home will play an important part in your child's learning.

Program / Register

Pointers within stage 3 of NSW English and Outcomes document have been set for each activity. Work in each unit has been designed to develop competence in the areas of Reading, Writing, Talking and Listening, Grammar and Spelling. A variety of text types has been covered to develop understanding and interest in language. There is provision for simple registration of each lesson.

Page	Strand	Level	Pointers	Reg.
			Term 1 Unit 1 - Friends and Family	
12	Spelling	3.11	• Uses knowledge of letter patterns and important parts of words to attempt to spell words. • Uses some spelling rules to spell unknown words (e.g. double letters). • Uses letters to represent all vowel and consonant sounds in a word. • Recognises common letter patterns and important parts of words. • Uses knowledge of word parts (suffixes).	
13	Talking and Listening	3.1 3.2	• Highlights important parts of events that are recounted in order. • Prepares and presents a detailed talk that is well organised.	
14	Reading	3.5 3.6	• Understands what is read at a literal level. • Understands what is read at an inferential level.	
15	Writing	3.9 3.10	• Clearly expresses ideas, feelings and events through writing poetry. • Tries to use language economically to produce ideas or images when creating poetry.	
16	Proofreading	3.9 3.11	• Consistently makes educated attempts at spelling. • Complete a sentence cloze using a word bank.	
17	Grammar	3.10	• Correctly uses words that are often confused, (quiet, quite). • Identifies and uses common and proper nouns. • Correctly uses quotation marks in sentences.	
18	Reading	3.5 3.6	• Understands what is read at a literal level. • Understands what is read at an inferential level.	
19	Grammar	3.10	• Identifies verbs and understands their function.	
			Term 1 Unit 2 - Floating and Sinking	
20	Spelling	3.11	• Uses knowledge of letter patterns and important parts of words to attempt to spell words. • Uses some spelling rules to spell unknown words. • Uses letters to represent all vowel and consonant sounds in a word. • Recognises common letter patterns and important parts of words. • Uses knowledge of word parts (suffixes).	
21	Grammar Using Words	3.10	• Identifies, adds and corrects punctuation in a passage. • Matches words and meanings • Using words in sentences	
22	Reading	3.5 3.6	• Understands what is read at a literal level. • Understands what is read at an inferential level.	
23	Proofreading	3.9 3.11	• Consistently makes educated attempts at spelling. • Uses many strategies when spelling.	
24/ 25	Writing	3.9 3.10 3.14	• Gives a few related reasons to explain a common phenomenon. • Makes a set of steps or instructions with attention to detail and logical structure. • Explains in some detail a common phenomenon. • Writes a set of explicit instructions that involve related steps.	

Page	Strand	Level	Pointers	Reg.
26	Talking & Listening	3.1 3.2	• Highlights important parts of events that are recounted in order. • Prepares and presents a detailed talk that is well organised.	
27	Grammar	3.10	• Identifies antonyms of some words. • Uses prefixes to create antonyms. • Correctly uses words that are often confused. (came, come). • Identifies adjectives in sentences.	
			Term 1 Unit 3 - Australian Explorers	
28	Spelling	3.11	• Uses knowledge of letter patterns and important parts of words to attempt to spell words. • Uses some spelling rules to spell unknown words. • Uses letters to represent all vowel and consonant sounds in a word. • Recognises common letter patterns and important parts of words. • Uses knowledge of word parts (prefixes, suffixes, compound words).	
29	Talking and Listening	3.1 3.2 3.3 3.4	• Listens and discusses ideas with peers in problem-solving groups. • Gives a brief report to the class on a group discussion. • Tries to persuade others in the class to a point of view or action by giving a few reasons. • Attempts to use strategies for effectively taking part in structured small group activities. • Presents a strong point of view, offering some logical reasons or arguments. • Listens carefully and responds constructively to the points of view of others in group discussions. • Prepares and presents an accurate summation of decisions reached in group discussions. • Uses strategies to help small group discussions.	
30	Reading	3.5 3.6	• Constructs a timeline to show the correct sequence of events.	
31	Proofreading	3.9 3.11	• Consistently makes educated attempts at spelling. • Uses many strategies when spelling.	
32	Reading	3.5 3.6	• Understands what is read at a literal level. • Understands what is read at an inferential level.	
33	Grammar	3.10	• Adds detail to make sentences more interesting. • Correctly punctuates sentences using capital letters and full stops. • Locates antonyms for given words. • Correctly uses words that are often confused, (very, real).	
34	Grammar	3.10	• Identifies sentences as Statements, Commands or Questions. • Correctly uses commas to separate a series of things. • Matches words with their meanings.	
35	Writing	3.9 3.10	• Constructs a recount putting in order several aspects of an event. • Constructs a recount reflecting on and describing events in detail.	
			Term 1 Unit 4 - Narrative Tutorial	
36-39	Writing / Grammar Reading/Writing (Modelling)	3.10 3.9 3.10	• Change text to past tense. • Identifies and uses action verbs in sentences. • Completes information about a well known narrative • Writes an imaginary story with a clear storyline in which some events are clearly related to the resolution of a problem. • Reads a narrative, then completes an analysis plan. • Writes a story in which ideas, details and events are developed and related to the storyline.	

5

Page	Strand	Level	Pointers	Reg.
			Term 2 Unit 1 - Narrative - The Wheelchair	
40	Spelling	3.11	• Uses knowledge of letter patterns and important parts of words to attempt to spell words. • Uses some spelling rules to spell unknown words (e.g. double letters). • Uses letters to represent all vowel and consonant sounds in a word. • Recognises common letter patterns and important parts of words. • Uses knowledge of word parts (prefixes, suffixes, compound words).	
41	Reading	3.6	• Reads independently using self-correction strategies. • Reads silently and discusses what has been read.	
42	Reading	3.5 3.6	• Understands what is read at a literal level. • Understands what is read at an inferential level.	
43	Proofreading	3.9 3.11	• Consistently makes educated attempts at spelling. • Uses many strategies when spelling.	
44/ 45	Writing	3.9 3.10 3.14	• Discusses both sides of an issue in writing by raising some relevant points. • Discusses both sides of an issue in writing and tries to relate them to one another.	
46	Reading	3.8	• Identifies the setting of the story.	
47	Grammar	3.10	• Correctly edits a passage for spelling and punctuation. • Correctly identifies and uses adverbs in sentences. • Locates synonyms for given words.	
			Term 2 Unit 2 - Space	
48	Spelling	3.11	• Uses knowledge of letter patterns and important parts of words to attempt to spell words. • Uses some spelling rules to spell unknown words (e.g. double letters). • Uses letters to represent all vowel and consonant sounds in a word. • Recognises common letter patterns and important parts of words. • Uses knowledge of word parts (prefixes, suffixes, compound words).	
49	Talking and Listening	3.1 3.2 3.3 3.4	• Listens and discusses ideas with peers in problem-solving groups. • Gives a brief report to the class on a group discussion. • Tries to persuade others in the class to a point of view or action, by giving a few reasons. • Attempts to use strategies for effectively taking part in structured small group activities. • Presents a strong point of view, offering some logical reasons or arguments. • Listens carefully and responds constructively to the points of view of others in group discussions. • Prepares and presents an accurate summation of decisions reached in group discussions. • Uses strategies to help small group discussions.	
50	Grammar	3.10	• Correctly uses conjunctions to join two sentences.	
50/51	Writing	3.9 3.10	• Writes an imaginary story with a clear storyline in which some events are clearly related to the resolution of a problem. • Writes a story in which ideas, details and events are developed and related to the storyline.	

Page	Strand	Level	Pointers	Reg.
52	Reading	3.6	• Makes brief notes of information and research. • Makes more detailed notes of information.	
53	Proofreading	3.9 3.11	• Consistently makes educated attempts at spelling. • Uses many strategies when spelling.	
54	Grammar	3.10	• Identifies and corrects punctuation errors. • Correctly uses words that are often confused (took, taken), (spoke, spoken).	
55	Reading	3.5 3.6	• Understands what is read at a literal level. • Understands what is read at an inferential level.	
			Term 2 Unit 3 - Newspapers	
56	Spelling	3.11	• Uses knowledge of letter patterns and important parts of words to attempt to spell words. • Uses some spelling rules to spell unknown words (e.g. double letters). • Uses letters to represent all vowel and consonant sounds in a word. • Recognises common letter patterns and important parts of words. • Uses knowledge of word parts (prefixes, suffixes, compound words).	
57	Reading	3.5 3.6	• Understands what is read at a literal level. • Understands what is read at an inferential level.	
58	Talking and Listening	3.1 3.3	• Briefly interviews others to gain information about an issue. • Actively listens to a speaker by attempting to recognise the topic and focus by asking relevant questions. • Gains information about an issue by interviewing others using probing questions requiring answers in some detail. • Listens carefully and responds positively to other points of view.	
59	Writing	3.9 3.10 3.14	• Writes an editorial giving a few related reasons that support a position. • Argues in writing a position or point of view raising relevant points in support of an issue.	
60	Grammar	3.10	• Correctly uses speech marks in a written conversation. • Uses better words for "get" or "gets". • Correctly uses words that are often confused, (past, passed).	
61	Reading	3.5 3.6	• Understands what is read at a literal level. • Understands what is read at an inferential level.	
62	Proofreading Cloze Passage	3.9 3.11 3.7	• Consistently makes educated attempts at spelling. • Uses many strategies when spelling. • Uses contextual clues to answer cloze passages.	
63	Grammar	3.10	• Uses alliteration in sentences. • Identifies action verbs in sentences. • Rewrites sentences to indicate past tense.	
			Term 2 Unit 4 - Argument Tutorial	
64	Grammar	3.10	• Correctly uses conjunctions to join two sentences. • Uses strong emotive words in a passage.	
65	Reading and Writing	3.9 3.10 3.14	• Read the presented argument, then discuss. • Writes an argument giving a few related reasons that support a position. • Argues in writing a position or point of view raising relevant points in support of an issue.	

Page	Strand	Level	Pointers	Reg.
			Term 3 Unit 1 - Narrative - The Mild Colonial Boy	
66	Spelling	3.11	• Uses knowledge of letter patterns and important parts of words to attempt to spell words. • Uses some spelling rules to spell unknown words (e.g. double letters). • Uses letters to represent all vowel and consonant sounds in a word. • Recognises common letter patterns and important parts of words. • Uses knowledge of word parts (prefixes, suffixes, compound words).	
67	Reading	3.6	• Reads independently using self-correction strategies. • Reads silently and discusses what has been read.	
68	Proofreading	3.9 3.11	• Consistently makes educated attempts at spelling. • Uses many strategies when spelling.	
69	Writing	3.9 3.10	• Constructs a media recount, putting many of the events in order. • Constructs a media recount containing a headline, stating the facts in order and putting forward a point of view.	
70	Grammar	3.10	• Correctly uses speech marks in a written conversation. • Forms contractions by joining two words together. • Uses verbs and adverbs to describe nouns.	
71	Talking and Listening	3.1 3.3	• Briefly interviews others to gain information about an issue. • Actively listens to a speaker by attempting to recognise the topic and focus by asking relevant questions. • Gains information about an issue by interviewing others using probing questions requiring answers in some detail. • Listens carefully and responds positively to other points of view.	
72	Writing	3.5 3.9	• Constructs a "Wanted" poster to show aspects of a character from a text.	
73	Grammar	3.10	• Uses better words for "said". • Selects and uses appropriate adverbs in a passage. • Identifies and uses correct homonyms in a sentence.	
			Term 3 Unit 2 - Bushrangers	
74	Spelling	3.11	• Uses knowledge of letter patterns and important parts of words to attempt to spell words. • Uses some spelling rules to spell unknown words (e.g. double letters). • Uses letters to represent all vowel and consonant sounds in a word. • Recognises common letter patterns and important parts of words. • Uses knowledge of word parts (prefixes, suffixes, compound words).	
75	Grammar	3.10	• Correctly uses words that are often confused. • Identifies synonyms from a group of words. • Locates antonyms for given words. • Identifies suitable adjectives to describe nouns. • Selects and uses appropriate adverbs for given sentences.	
76/ 77	Writing	3.9 3.10 3.14	• Writes a report which includes information on several aspects of the topic. • Constructs an information report in detail on some aspects of the topic.	
78/ 79	Reading	3.5 3.6	• Understands what is read at a literal level. • Complete a simple comprehension. • Understands what is read at an inferential level. • Constructs a timeline to show the correct sequence of events.	
80	Proofreading	3.9 3.11	• Consistently makes educated attempts at spelling. • Uses many strategies when spelling.	
	Cloze Passage	3.7	• Uses contextual clues to complete cloze passages.	

Page	Strand	Level	Pointers	Reg.
81	Grammar	310	• Uses capital letters in sentences. • Identifies appropriate collective nouns. • Uses commas to indicate pauses and to separate parts of sentences.	
			Term 3 Unit 3 - Endangered Animals	
82	Spelling	3.11	• Uses knowledge of letter patterns and important parts of words to attempt to spell words. • Uses some spelling rules to spell unknown words (e.g. double letters). • Uses letters to represent all vowel and consonant sounds in a word. • Recognises common letter patterns and important parts of words. • Uses knowledge of word parts (prefixes, suffixes, compound words).	
83	Reading	3.6	• Locates information from a text and makes brief notes. • Locates information that is important to the purpose for reading and makes more detailed notes.	
84	Grammar	3.10	• Identifies the correct pronouns in a passage. • Correctly uses conjunctions to join two sentences. • Locates antonyms and synonyms for given words.	
85	Writing	3.9 3.10 3.14	• Constructs and writes an information report in detail on a number of aspects of the topic.	
86	Proofreading Reading	3.9 3.11 3.5 3.6	• Consistently makes educated attempts at spelling. • Uses many strategies when spelling. • Understands what is read at a literal level. • Understands what is read at an inferential level.	
87	Grammar	3.10	• Uses commas to indicate a pause and to separate parts of sentences. • Identifies and corrects punctuation errors in a passage. • Correctly uses words that are often confused. (went, gone).	
88	Talking and Listening	3.1 3.2 3.3 3.4	• Listens and discusses ideas with peers in problem-solving groups. • Gives a brief report to the class on a group discussion. • Tries to persuade others in the class to a point of view or action by giving a few reasons. • Attempts to use strategies for effectively taking part in structured small group activities. • Presents a strong point of view, offering some logical reasons or arguments. • Listens carefully and responds constructively to the points of view of others in group discussions. • Prepares and presents an accurate summation of decisions reached in group discussions. • Uses strategies to help small group discussions.	
89	Writing	3.9 3.10 3.14	• Discusses both sides of an issue in writing by raising some relevant points. • Discusses both sides of an issue in writing and tries to relate them to one another.	
			Term 3 Unit 4 - Information Report Tutorial	
90	Grammar	3.10	• Changes text to present tense. • Uses appropriate relational verbs in sentences.	
91	Reading	3.9 3.10 3.14	• Reads a detailed information report containing a number of aspects of the topic.	

Page	Strand	Level	Pointers	Reg.
			Term 4 Unit 1 - The Human Body	
92	Spelling	3.11	• Uses knowledge of letter patterns and important parts of words to attempt to spell words. • Uses some spelling rules to spell unknown words (e.g. double letters). • Uses letters to represent all vowel and consonant sounds in a word. • Recognises common letter patterns and important parts of words. • Uses knowledge of word parts (prefixes, suffixes, compound words).	
93	Grammar	3.10	• Correctly uses conjunctions to join two sentences. • Uses correct punctuation in sentences. • Locates synonyms and antonyms for given words.	
94	Reading	3.5 3.6	• Understands what is read at a literal level. • Understands what is read at an inferential level.	
95	Proofreading Reading - Comprehension	3.9 3.11 3.5 3.6	• Consistently makes educated attempts at spelling. • Uses many strategies when spelling. • Understands what is read at a literal level. • Understands what is read at an inferential level.	
96	Grammar	3.10	• Correctly uses apostrophes to shorten words. • Correctly uses words that are often confused, (good, well), (wrote, written), (there, their, they're).	
97	Reading	3.5 3.6	• Understands what is read at a literal level. • Understands what is read at an inferential level.	
98/ 99	Writing	3.9 3.10 3.14	• Predicts the outcome of an experiment. • Writes a set of steps or instructions with some attention to detail and logical structure that involve related steps. • Explains in some detail a common phenomenon.	
			Term 4 Unit 2 - Food and Nutrition	
100	Spelling	3.11	• Uses knowledge of letter patterns and important parts of words to attempt to spell words. • Uses some spelling rules to spell unknown words (e.g. double letters). • Uses letters to represent all vowel and consonant sounds in a word. • Recognises common letter patterns and important parts of words. • Uses knowledge of word parts (prefixes, suffixes, compound words).	
101	Talking and Listening	3.3 3.2 3.4 3.1	• Presents mostly relevant, organised information on a debate topic to a group. • Tries to persuade peers to a point of view or action by presenting a few reasons. • Lists and organises main ideas on cue cards before debating. • Uses gestures and facial expressions to convey responses and emotions and to emphasise meaning. • Uses pause and repetition to emphasise spoken language. • Prepares, selects, orders and organises subject matter clearly for debate. • Presents a detailed point of view in spoken presentations. • Speaks clearly using pace, volume, pronunciation, enunciation and stress to improve meaning. • Listens carefully and constructively responds to opposing points of view on a familiar issue.	
102	Grammar	3.10	• Correctly uses conjunctions to join two sentences. • Identifies prefixes that affect the meaning of a word.	

Page	Strand	Level	Pointers	Reg.
103	Proofreading Reading - Comprehension	3.9 3.11 3.5 3.6	• Consistently makes educated attempts at spelling. • Uses many strategies when spelling. • Understands what is read at a literal level. • Understands what is read at an inferential level.	
104	Writing	3.9 3.10	• Write a set of steps or instructions with some attention to detail and logical structure. • Makes a set of explicit instructions that involve related steps.	
105	Reading	3.5 3.6	• Understands what is read at a literal level. • Understands what is read at an inferential level.	
106	Grammar	3.10	• Correctly uses the apostrophe to show possession. • Uses correct punctuation in given sentences. (capital letters, full stops, commas and apostrophes).	
107	Reading Cloze Passage	3.8 3.7	• Correctly sequences instructions in a text. • Uses contextual clues to complete a cloze passage.	
			Term 4 Unit 3 - Narrative - No Home	
108	Spelling	3.11	• Uses knowledge of letter patterns and important parts of words to attempt to spell words. • Uses some spelling rules to spell unknown words (e.g. double letters). • Uses letters to represent all vowel and consonant sounds in a word. • Recognises common letter patterns and important parts of words. • Uses knowledge of word parts (prefixes, suffixes, compound words).	
109	Reading	3.6	• Reads independently using self-correction strategies. • Reads silently and discusses what has been read.	
110	Reading	3.5 3.6	• Understands what is read at a literal level. • Understands what is read at an inferential level.	
111	Talking and Listening	3.1 3.2	• Shows an awareness of narrative texts by telling stories. • Engages listeners through the telling of a narrative text.	
112	Writing	3.9 3.10	• Writes an imaginary story with a clear storyline in which some events are clearly related to the resolution of a problem. • Writes a story in which ideas, details and events are developed and related to the storyline.	
113	Proofreading	3.9 3.11	• Consistently makes educated attempts at spelling. • Uses many strategies when spelling.	
114	Reading/Writing	3.5	• Constructs a story map to show a sequence of events from a text.	
115	Grammar	3.10	• Locates synonyms and antonyms for given words. • Correctly uses conjunctions to join two sentences. • Correctly uses words that are often confused, (threw, through), (here, hear).	
			Term 4 Unit 4 - Procedure Tutorial	
116	Grammar	3.10	• Correctly identifies the action verbs in a procedural text. • Correctly identifies the common nouns and adverb in a procedural text.	
117	Writing (Modelling)	3.9 3.10	• Follows a set of steps or instructions with some attention to detail and logical structure. • Follows a set of explicit instructions that involve related steps.	

Read, discuss and study the word bank. Add some more theme words. Remember to LOOK, COVER, WRITE and CHECK when learning spelling.

talent	quality	unique	describe	appearance
hobby	success	esteem	positive	feelings
express	emotion	affection	relationship	interact
trust	tolerate	accept	problem	company
value	pressure	friend	family	influence
loyal	special	ability	respect	skill
_____	_____	_____	_____	_____

Activity 1

Write the meaning of each of the following words and use each in a sentence.

a) unique _____

_____

b) interact _____

_____

c) tolerate _____

_____

Activity 2

Break the following words into syllables.

a) influence _____   b) emotion _____   c) ability _____

d) relationship _____   e) special _____

Activity 3 - WORD RULE

When a short vowel is followed by more than one consonant, you *do not double* the last letter when adding **ED** or **ING,** e.g. knock - knocked, knocking. Practise these.

a) mark _____   _____

b) trust _____   _____

c) accept _____   _____

d) respect _____   _____

e) interact _____   _____

Activity 4 - Crack the Code

25 15 21 / 3 1 14 / 1 12 23 1 25 19 / 20 18 21 19 20 / 25 15 21 18 / 6 18 9 5 14 4.

_____

Text Type - Recount - My Life Story

Jot down information about your life story under the following headings and then recount this information to the rest of your class.

Birth - Life as a Baby

_____

_____

_____

_____

_____

_____

My Family

_____

_____

_____

_____

_____

_____

From Kindergarten to Year 5

_____

_____

_____

_____

_____

_____

My Friends

_____

_____

_____

_____

_____

18 Gum Leaf Place
Redbrook
NSW 2111
Australia

Dear Matsuo,

Hello, my name is Carlos Valdez and I am 11 years old. I would love you to be my pen friend because I have just completed a project about Japan and I would like to learn more about your country.

I was born in Spain in a city called Madrid. My parents decided to come to Australia when I was just 6 months old. They wanted a better life for us because it was very hard for my father and mother to find jobs in Spain.

We came by aeroplane and stayed at my Uncle Manuel's house for two weeks. We then moved to our present house at Redbrook. My parents quickly found jobs and I was looked after by my Aunt Lina.

My parents tell me that I was an adventurous baby, always crawling and exploring the house. They also tell me that I fell on a table and split my lip when I was two years old. I had to have three stitches.

I started Kindergarten when I was five years old. I remember painting funny pictures of my father and chasing my friend Colin in the playground. My report says that I was good at Reading and Writing.

When I was eight years old, we returned to Spain for a holiday. It was fantastic! I didn't know I had such a big family! I enjoyed watching the bull fights and playing street soccer with all the local boys.

I am now in Year 5 and I have many friends. I enjoy all types of sport especially Soccer and I spend my time playing computer games and roller blading.

I hope that you will tell me all about you when you write back.

Your friend,
Carlos Valdez

Answer all questions in full sentences.

1. Why does Carlos want Matsuo to be his pen friend? _____

_____

2. Why did Carlos' parents come to Australia? _____

_____

3. How do you know that Carlos was an adventurous baby? _____

_____

4. Do you think Carlos liked Kindergarten? Give reasons for your answer. _____

_____

5. Name two things that Carlos liked about his trip to Spain. _____

_____

An **acrostic** poem is one where each line starts with each letter of the title. For example, this poem is about boys.

Busy running, rolling and pushing.
Only boys like football.
You will often see them playing video games.
See them run when the girls arrive!

Write a similar poem about friends.

F _____

R _____

I _____

E _____

N _____

D _____

S _____

Cinquains are five-line poems. Each line of the poem has a certain number of syllables. Each line gives information about the title.

SYLLABLES	DESCRIPTION	EXAMPLE
2	title	Grandma
4	description of the title	Old and wrinkled
6	action	Sitting, knitting, chatting
8	feeling	Looking after me when I'm sick
2	another word for title	Great friend

Write two cinquains about family members or friends on the lines.

_____

_____

_____

_____

_____

_____

_____

Circle the words that you think have been spelt incorrectly. Write the correct spelling. There is one incorrect word on each line.

My family has always been very importent to me. When I was born, my parents took grate care of me. They made sure that I had good food and a clean nappie.

1. _____

2. _____

3. _____

As I grew older, they made sure that their values, morels and atitudes were passed on to me. I learnt how to say "please" and "thank you" and I was always palite when visiters came to our house.

4. _____

5. _____

6. _____

7. _____

During this pereod, I also learned how to co-operate with others. I had all the usual arguements with my brother and sister, but, gradualy I was able to play with them in a sensibal way.

8. _____

9. _____

10. _____

11. _____

I am thankful for all the guidence that my parents have given me. I know that becuase of them, I will become a responsable citizen who will be able to make a positive contrabution to our community.

12. _____

13. _____

14. _____

15. _____

Cloze Passage

Fill in each blank with a word from the word bank.

| because | each | old | usually | talented | class | fight | both |

My best friend's name is Ashley. He is in my _____ at school and he is eleven years _____. He is my best friend _____ we have the same interests and hobbies.

We _____ collect football cards and swap them with _____ other. Also, we love to play marbles. We _____ go into the playground at school and play marbles. We put five marbles each into a circle and then we try to knock them out with another marble. Ashley usually wins because he is a very _____ marbles player.

I like Ashley because we get along with each other. We never _____ or argue.

Quiet or Quite? Complete the following sentences using either "quiet" or "quite".

1. My friend Vince is very _____ in class.

2. I received _____ a good report from my teacher.

3. My Uncle Jeff is _____ a good cricketer.

4. It was a cool, still and _____ evening as we sat on the verandah.

5. "You must be very _____ or you will disturb the baby," stated Mum.

Common and Proper Nouns

Proper nouns are special names given to a particular person or place, e.g. Joseph Tomasz, Sydney, England, Mrs Fraser, Alice Springs. They all have capital letters.
Common nouns are words used to name an animal, a person, a place or a thing, e.g. player, sailor, dog, elephant, city, park, beach, box, pen, table, bicycle. Common nouns do not have capital letters.

Use each of the following common and proper nouns in a sentence.

Australia	drum	cinema	Mr Darby	monkey

1. _____

2. _____

3. _____

4. _____

5. _____

Quotation Marks

To show the actual words spoken by a speaker, we use quotation marks, e.g. "Cindy, would you like to come to the Easter Show with me?" I asked.
Rewrite these sentences using quotation marks and capital letters where necessary.

1. We will be leaving for our holidays in January, I told my friend.

_____

2. I said to my mother, that roller coaster was fantastic!

_____

3. Would you like to swim in my pool? asked Uncle Bruno.

_____

4. I said to Jeanie let's go to the shop and buy an ice cream.

_____

5. What a fantastic goal! I yelled from the grandstand.

_____

Violence Does Not Solve Problems

Violence is on the increase, both in real life and on TV. Despite the fact that we see a great deal of violence, it does not solve problems.

Firstly, gang violence is commonplace in many countries. If one member of a gang walks down the wrong street, it is possible that he or she will get shot, stabbed or beaten up. In retaliation, the other gang then attempts to get revenge by killing members of the opposing gang. Violence breeds violence. Nothing has been achieved. If the gang members are caught, they will go to prison.

Also, some people get into arguments and this may lead to violence and aggression. One or both parties could get hurt and end up in hospital. Furthermore, if the police are called, someone may be charged with assault. Has the problem been solved to everyone's satisfaction? I think not!

As well, children see many forms of violence in the media and believe that this is the way to solve problems. Fights can occur in the playground and disagreements may happen in games of schoolyard sports. But what happens to the children displaying such behaviour? They are punished for breaking the rules.

To conclude, it is important that people are educated to solve problems so that both parties are satisfied with the solution. Violence breeds violence and more problems will be caused through it.

Comprehension - Answer all questions in full sentences.

1. Give a reason from the passage why gang members might get attacked.

   _____

2. Name two things that might happen if people become violent during an argument.

   _____

3. Give a reason from the passage why children are sometimes violent.

   _____

4. What happens to children who display aggressive behaviour in school?

   _____

5. What message is the author trying to give you, as the reader?

   _____

Grammar - Verbs

Sentences tell us about something that is happening. The part that tells us what is happening is called a verb. Verbs are about doing, feeling and thinking. The following sentence shows something that is happening: *My Dad hurt his thumb with a hammer.*

The verb in this sentence is **hurt**. This verb tells us about something that was done. It tells about an action in the sentence.

Find out what is happening in the following sentences and write the verb opposite.

1. Grandpa walks very slowly down to the shops. _____

2. The wind slammed the door shut. _____

3. The new student felt lonely. _____

4. My friend swam in dangerous waters. _____

5. Trinh and I played sensibly. _____

Some **verbs** tell us what things are or what they have, e.g. Jeremy **is** my best friend. Marco **has** a new pair of jeans.

Read the following sentences, then identify and write the verb for each sentence.

1. Grandma is a very friendly lady. _____

2. He dragged the bucket of sand. _____

3. Lily sprinted to the finish line. _____

4. My family has a tidy house. _____

5. My friends are in Year 6. _____

Read the following text, then underline the verbs. Write them in the lists below.

My friends have many interests. We walk down to the river and fish for tadpoles. We are hot, so we sit in the shade of a tree and eat ice cream. At the end of the day we have no energy but we have smiles on our faces

Verbs	Verbs

Read, discuss and study the word bank. Add some more theme words. Remember to LOOK, COVER, WRITE and CHECK when learning spelling.

design	materials	equipment	procedure	result
conclusion	experiment	plastic	container	alter
float	properties	objects	variety	record
predict	investigate	important	dissolve	expand
equal	amount	water	level	construct
measure	report	observe	discuss	collect
_____	_____	_____	_____	_____
_____	_____	_____	_____	_____

Activity 1

Build on the given base words by adding the endings in the table (Watch your spelling!) An example has been given.

Base word	Add s	Add ed	Add ing	Suffix
design	designs	designed	designing	designer
predict	_____	_____	_____	_____
observe	_____	_____	_____	_____
discuss	_____	_____	_____	_____
construct	_____	_____	_____	_____

Activity 2

Underline the five words of more than one syllable that are hidden in each string of letters.

a) hifamountshenygmeasurepledexpandynfojinvestigateorfdlipeplasticaheboklioj

b) defwequaloklokcollecteeargijujilklevelnuimyuilowaterrecsuhexperimentyceda

Activity 3 - WORD RULE

To make nouns plural (more than one) add -S, e.g enter - enters. Practise these.

a) design _____ b) float _____ c) equal _____

d) measure _____ e) level _____ f) amount _____

g) collect _____ h) alter _____ i) observe _____

Activity 4 - FUN SPOT - SPELLING BINGO

Select nine words from the list at the top of the page and write them on the bingo grid. Play Spelling Bingo!

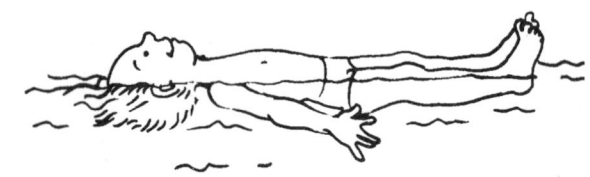

Rewrite the following passage in the space below and add punctuation where necessary. (There are no spelling mistakes!)

By looking at an object we can sometimes tell whether it will float or sink a feather will probably float but something like a marble will sink there are other objects that may float first but if we do something to them they may sink for example a dry sponge may float on water while a wet sponge may sink

_____

_____

_____

_____

_____

Word Meanings

Match the word in Box B with its meaning in Box A.

Box A	Box B
to examine closely	predict
a way of doing something	record
having great meaning	investigate
to tell the future	important
to write down information	procedure

Off, Of or From?

Complete each sentence by writing *off, of* or *from*.

1. She dived _____ the diving board.

2. The burglar ran _____ the house.

3. Please cut two slices _____ bread.

4. Take the sharp knife _____ the little boy.

5. Did you learn anything _____ the lesson?

6. You may borrow it _____ me if you like.

7. You must keep _____ the new lawn.

8. May I have one _____ your lollies?

9. We have just received a parcel _____ our relatives.

10. You may have half _____ my chocolate.

How To Make A Boat That Floats

What you will need

- A bowl or tub of water
- An empty soft drink bottle (at least 1.25L)
- A drinking straw
- Blu-Tac or plasticine
- A4 sheet of cardboard
- A pair of scissors or Stanley knife
- An electric fan

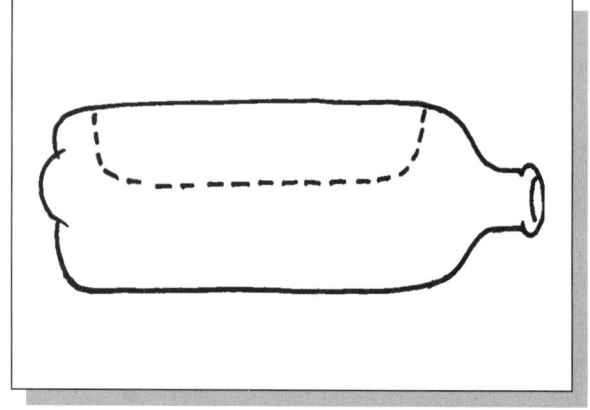

Procedure

1. Using the scissors or Stanley knife, cut out a rectangular section of plastic as shown. (You may require a teacher or an adult to supervise you.) This will give you the basic boat shape.
2. Using the sheet of cardboard, cut out your own design of a sail.
3. Attach the sail to the drinking straw (mast) with Blu-Tac or plasticine.
4. Place some Blu-Tac or plasticine in the bottom of your boat and attach your drinking straw to it.
5. Add water to your bowl or tub so that it is three-quarters full.
6. Test the buoyancy of your boat by placing it in the bowl or tub.
7. Use an electric fan to move your boat along the water.

Comprehension

Answer all questions in full sentences.

1. Why do you think that adult supervision is required in the making of this boat?

_____

_____

2. What do you do with the sheet of cardboard? _____

_____

3. What do you think is meant by "Test the buoyancy of your boat..."?

_____

_____

4. With what do you stick the sail to the straw? _____

_____

5. What could you do to your boat if it sinks when you test it?

_____

_____

Circle the words that you think have been spelt incorrectly. Write each word correctly. There is one incorrect word for each line.

Submarines are unusual but special floating vessles

because they are able to sink and also retern to the

surfase of the water if required.

1. _____

2. _____

3. _____

Ballast tanks have controll over how deep they dive. To

alow the submarine to sink, the tanks are filled with

water. To enabel the submarine to rise, the water is

pumped out of the tank and replased with air.

4. _____

5. _____

6. _____

7. _____

The hovercraft is one of the most amazeing inventions

of the twentieth century. It has the abilerty to travel on

both land and water.

8. _____

9. _____

The enjins suck in air and pump it downward. This makes

a cushon of air that stops the hovercraft from touching

the surface it is traveling over. This gives passengers an

extremely smooth jurney.

10. _____

11. _____

12. _____

13. _____

Cloze Passage

Fill each blank with a word from the word bank.

water	boat	speeds	through	very	push	flow	move

Many boats and ships have propellers which they use to _____ them

along the water. The propeller cuts _____ the water and pushes it back

behind the vessel. This pushing of _____ behind the vessel enables the

vessel to _____ forward.

A jet-propelled _____ is able to travel at high _____

without the use of a propeller. The jet causes a fast moving _____ of

water which pushes the boat along _____ quickly.

Science Experiment - Floating and Sinking

- Investigate to find out which objects will float and which objects will sink.
- Make sure that the objects you use are brought in or can be located in a classroom.
- Test each object.
- Discuss with your group what happens after you test each object.

Here are some pictures of the sorts of objects you may wish to test.

On the next page is space to write up your experiment.

- The Aim of your experiment should tell what you were trying to find out by doing the experiment.
- The Equipment section is where you list all the equipment you use for this experiment.
- The Procedure section should list in order all the things you did during the experiment.
- The Results section is where you write down your observations (i.e. what happened).
- The Conclusion is where you answer your aim (i.e. from the experiment what did you find out?).

Draw your results from the experiment in this box.

Experiment - Floating and Sinking

Aim: _____

_____

_____

Equipment: _____

_____

_____

Procedure:

1. _____
2. _____
3. _____
4. _____
5. _____
6. _____
7. _____
8. _____
9. _____
10. _____

Results: _____

_____

_____

_____

_____

_____

_____

_____

_____

Conclusion: _____

_____

_____

_____

After completing the experiment on Floating and Sinking, plan, prepare and practise giving an oral report on your findings. When presenting your report, remember to:

- Make eye contact with your audience.
- Use palm cards if necessary (write the information in point form).
- Speak clearly and with good volume.
- Make your voice interesting (emphasise words, vary your volume and tone of voice).
- Stand up straight.
- Use hand gestures where possible.

The sentence starters below will help you to plan and prepare your report.

- Our group has completed an experiment about _____

_____

- The equipment we used was _____

_____

_____

- For this experiment, we had to _____

_____

_____

_____

_____

_____

- The results of the experiment show that _____

_____

- The experiment proves that _____

_____

_____

_____

Words that are opposite in meaning are called *antonyms*. Write the antonyms of the following words.

1. start _____   2. rough _____   3. fast _____

4. hard _____   5. far _____   6. young _____

7. rise _____   8. forget _____   9. love _____

Prefixes - to form Antonyms

A prefix is a word part put in front of a word to change the meaning. Some prefixes can be used to form antonyms. For example,

   polite - impolite (prefix is **im**)   capable - incapable (prefix is **in**)
   happy - unhappy (prefix is **un**)   appear - disappear (prefix is **dis**)

Form antonyms for the following words by using one of the prefixes above.

1. do _____   2. agree _____   3. perfect _____

4. able _____   5. correct _____   6. qualify _____

7. direct _____   8. possible_____   9. usual _____

Came or Come?

Complete each sentence by writing *came* or *come*.

1. Can you tell me why he hasn't _____?

2. Jan _____ as quickly as she could.

3. I will _____ to visit you in hospital.

4. Raj has _____ to help me with my homework.

5. Our uncle _____ over to watch the television.

Adjectives

Adjectives are words that describe nouns, e.g. playful dog (*playful* describes the dog). In the following sentences, identify the adjective and the noun that it describes.

1. The strong wind blew the tree down.   _____ describes _____

2. The noisy crowd roared with approval.   _____ describes _____

3. Thao's handwriting is neat.   _____ describes _____

4. A scary ghost flew past our faces.   _____ describes _____

5. Mum stared at the untidy bedroom.   _____ describes _____

Read, discuss and study the word bank. Add some more theme words. Remember to LOOK, COVER, WRITE and CHECK when learning spelling.

navigate crew explore discover voyage achieve _____	Australia mountain accompany survey botanist chart _____	downstream · agricultural grazing companion supplies equipment _____	descent pioneer expedition travel · settlement scurvy _____	vast · frustrated disaster violence direction · endured _____

Activity 1

Find the meaning of the following words and then use each in a sentence.

a) endured _____

_____

b) companion _____

_____

c) descent _____

_____

Activity 2

Build on the given base words by adding the endings in the table. (Watch your spelling!) An example has been given.

Base word	Add -s	Add -ed	Add -ing	Suffix
navigate	navigates	navigated	navigating	navigation
explore	_____	_____	_____	_____
survey	_____	_____	_____	_____
accompany	_____	_____	_____	_____
travel	_____	_____	_____	_____

Activity 3

Find complete words inside the ones given, e.g. palace - lace, pal.

1. navigate _____
2. discover _____
3. voyage _____
4. achieve _____
5. mountain _____
6. accompany _____
7. chart _____
8. agricultural _____
9. equipment _____
10. settlement _____
11. direction _____
12. endured _____

Activity 4 - FUN SPOT

Make as many word as you can. You must use the bold letter in all words that you make.

r	t	s
e	**i**	k
l	c	n

_____ _____ _____ _____ _____

_____ _____ _____ _____ _____

_____ _____ _____ _____ _____

Going on an Expedition

Your group of four is going to explore a part of Australia. Each of you is going to carry a backpack. From the list of items, **choose six** items that you believe are essential for this expedition. Just in case you can't take all six items, (there may not be enough room in your backpacks), rank your chosen items in order, giving reasons for your choice. Make sure that your group agrees on all the choices that have been made. Be prepared to have your reporter report the group's choices to the rest of the class.

CHOOSE FROM THESE ITEMS

Tents	Camp Beds	Hats	Empty Bottles	Water
Guns	Knife	Boots	Dried Food	Map
Frying Pan	Billy	Binoculars	Flour	Compass

Item No.1   Reasons _____

Item No.2   Reasons _____

Item No.3   Reasons _____

Item No.4   Reasons _____

Item No.5   Reasons _____

Item No.6   Reasons _____

Tasmania was originally called Van Diemen's Land. In 1853, the name was changed to Tasmania because the colony had become self-governing and the convicts had stopped coming.

Because Tasmania is such a small island, most of the journeys made by explorers were short. However, some of these journeys were difficult because of the harsh land, steep mountains, dense bush and fast rivers.

In 1793, Lieutenant John Hayes named the Derwent River and George Harris sailed the Huon River in 1804. Lieutenant Thomas Laycock became the first person to cross Van Diemen's Land when he travelled from Port Dalrymple to Hobart. Charles Grimes followed the Jordan Valley, crossing the island from south to north. In 1815-16, James Kelly and four companions circumnavigated the island in a whaleboat. On the west coast, Kelly gave Macquarie Harbour its name. In 1819-20, Henry Rice explored much of the east coast, discovering some good farming land. James Hobbs and twelve convicts explored the west coast in two whaleboats in 1824. They came across dense bush and steep mountains inland.

Henry Hellyer explored the north-west of Tasmania in 1827. He named many places such as Hampshire Hills and St. Valentine's Peak. In the same year, Joseph Fossey trekked overland from Launceston to Emu Bay (now called Burnie).

Construct a timeline showing the exploration of Tasmania.

Timeline of Tasmania's Explorers

Year	Name of Explorer and what he did
1793	
1804	
1807	
1807	
1815 - 16	
1819 - 20	
1824	
1827	
1827	

Circle the words that you think have been spelt incorrectly. Write the correct spelling. There is one incorrect word on each line.

Robert O'Hara Burke and William Wills became the furst

explorers to cross Austraila from south to north.

In 1860 they commensed their journey with seventeen other

men.

1. _____

2. _____

3. _____

Burke was not an experenced bushman but he was given

the job of leading the expediton to the north. Wills was

apointed as astronomer and surveyor for the trip. He loved

the bush and was skiled in bushcraft. He was also good at

keeping detaled records.

4. _____

5. _____

6. _____

7. _____

8. _____

The men choosen to go on the trip knew little about the

climate or landscape of the area but the organisors were

very well equiped for the trip.

9. _____

10. _____

11. _____

Arrangments were rushed because the organisers were

aware that the South Australian Goverment intended to send

John McDouall Stuart on a simlar trip.

12. _____

13. _____

14. _____

Cloze Passage

Fill in each blank with a word from the word bank.

| inland | solve | following | mystery | named | English | explored | rivers |

Charles Sturt arrived in Australia in 1826. He was an _____ military officer. He was fascinated by the mystery of the _____ sea. He wanted to find out if the _____ flowed into the inland sea. In 1828, he decided to try and _____ the mystery.

Firstly, after _____ the Macquarie River, he found and _____ the Darling River but came no closer to solving the _____.

He also _____ the Murrumbidgee and Murray Rivers.

Wylie - An Aboriginal Explorer

It is not known where or when Wylie was born, or what
he did in his early life. However, in 1840 Wylie joined Edward
John Eyre on his expedition to find a route west across the
Nullarbor Plain. He, along with two other Aboriginal men,
Neremberein and Cootachah helped Eyre and John Baxter
to find waterholes in the area. The water holes were sometimes
three hundred kilometres apart but the five men struggled on.

There was a loud blast on the morning of the 29th April. Wylie discovered Baxter in a
pool of blood and realised that Neremberein and Cootachah had gone, taking with
them most of the food, firearms and ammunition.

Eyre and Wylie battled on through barren land, coping with the few provisions they had
left. They became so weak that frequent rests were necessary.

Almost a year after leaving Adelaide, Wylie and Eyre spotted a ship above a headland.
They fired their guns and lit a fire to attract attention.

The Captain of the French whaler took them aboard and looked after them until they
were well enough to continue their journey to Albany, a 450-kilometre hike.

Eyre and Wylie arrived in Albany in torrential rain. Wylie stayed in the west and became a
local celebrity.

Comprehension

Answer all questions in full sentences.

1. How many people went on this expedition? _____

   _____

2. Give two reasons why the expedition was difficult. _____

   _____

   _____

3. What happened to John Baxter? _____

   _____

4. What is meant by "coping with the few provisions they had left"? _____

   _____

5. What did Wylie do after the expedition? _____

   _____

Grammar - Interesting Sentences

Add detail to the following sentences to make them more interesting. For example,
- a) Blaxland, Lawson and Wentworth found a way through the Blue Mountains.
- b) Despite a struggle, Blaxland, Lawson and Wentworth discovered a route through the Blue Mountains.

1. Oxley and his men loaded the boats and sailed away.

_____

2. John Oxley had two boats and a large crew.

_____

3. Hume and Hovell had an argument and split up.

_____

4. Thomas Mitchell was a difficult person who quickly made enemies.

_____

Full Stops and Capital Letters

Rewrite the following sentences using capital letters and full stops.
1. john septimus roe explored the south coast of western australia

_____

2. ludwig leichhardt arrived in sydney and wanted to explore central australia

_____

3. charles sturt was always friendly towards aboriginal people

_____

4. william hovell was a farmer and ex-sea captain

_____

5. hamilton hume spent his childhood exploring the area around berrima

_____

Antonyms

Give an antonym (opposite) for each of these words.

1. asleep _____ 2. fail _____

3. fast _____ 4. loud _____

5. after _____ 6. defend _____

7. come _____ 8. grow _____

Very or Real?

Complete the following sentences using either "very" or "real".

1. The cartoon we watched was _____ good.

2. I ate a _____ tasty meat pie.

3. The drink was made of _____ oranges.

33

Statements are sentences that tell us about something that happened. They end with full stops.

Questions are sentences that ask for information. They end with question marks.

Commands are sentences that give a command or order. They usually end with full stops except when they are spoken with great feeling; they then end with exclamation marks.

Read the sentences and identify them as Statements, Questions or Commands.

1. John McDouall Stuart started work as a surveyor. _____

2. When was John McDouall Stuart born? _____

3. "Get out of my way!" yelled Thomas Mitchell. _____

4. George was an extremely intelligent man. _____

5. How did Edmund Kennedy die? _____

Commas

Commas are used to mark off a series of nouns, e.g. *We saw some red, orange, blue and purple flowers.*

Rewrite the following sentences. Include commas where necessary.

1. Ludwig Leichhardt was interested in Australia's rocks plants and animals.

_____

2. Edward John Eyre found Lakes Torrens Eyre Blanche Calabonna and Frome.

_____

3. Hamilton Hume travelled with John Oxley James Meehan and Charles Throsby.

_____

4. George Evans was an artist teacher writer bushman bookseller and explorer.

_____

5. A way through the Blue Mountains was found by Blaxland Lawson and Wentworth.

_____

One Word for Several

Draw a line from each sentence to one word that means the same or similar.

1. unable to be passed   versatile

2. able to do a variety of things   drought

3. a long period of dry weather   impassable

4. a journey made for a special purpose   botanist

5. one who studies plants   expedition

Select an inland explorer. Write a diary recount of one of his expeditions. Imagine you are the explorer and explain how you feel about the things that happened to you.

Explorer's Diary

_____

_____

_____

_____

_____

_____

_____

_____

_____

_____

_____

_____

_____

_____

_____

_____

_____

_____

Draw and label an event that occurred on your travels.

Definition

Narratives tell a story. They give us a view of the world and entertain and instruct the reader or listener.

Features

Narratives:

- use specific nouns which can be human or animal (sometimes things).
- use joining words such as *afterwards, meanwhile, in the end, first to do with time.*
- are usually in the past tense (though this can change during the story).
- indicate what characters are thinking, feeling and saying.
- use a variety of action verbs such as *running, hoped, blasted, screaming, coming.*

Activities - Past Tense

Change the following sentences using past tense verbs.

1. She will travel to Melbourne to buy new tools.

   _____

2. Maurice will dive spectacularly to save the shot.

   _____

3. The car flies around the corner at great speed.

   _____

4. He will stumble and fall as he tries to escape.

   _____

5. Jane will sack the worker because he is dishonest.

   _____

Action Verbs

Add action verbs to the following sentences.

1. The young child _____ when he saw the poisonous spider.

2. Our mother _____ when the rat came into view.

3. A neighbour _____ with pleasure when he found out that he had won Lotto.

4. The car _____ out of control and hit a power pole.

5. A bottle of soft drink _____ when my friend shook it.

6. Grandma _____ me to stay at her house for another day.

7. The officer in charge _____ his men to load their rifles.

8. A grateful man _____ his rescuers for saving his life.

Examples of Narratives

Look at the example of "Jack and the Beanstalk" and complete the information for the two incomplete narratives.

Jack and the Beanstalk

Orientation

Characters

Jack

Strange man

Jack's mother

Giant

Giant's wife

What: Jack takes the cow to sell at the market because he and his mother are poor.

When: Early one morning.

Where: In a town.

Complication

Events

- Jack swaps the cow for some beans that are owned by a strange man.
- Jack's mother angrily throws the beans out of the window when she finds out what Jack did.
- Beans grow into a beanstalk overnight.
- Jack climbs beanstalk and goes to Giant's house.
- Jack steals things from Giant.
- Giant chases Jack.

Resolution

- Jack scrambles down beanstalk.
- Jack chops down beanstalk.
- Giant falls from beanstalk and dies.
- Jack and his mother are rich for the rest of their lives.

Cinderella

Orientation
Characters

_____

_____

_____

_____

What: _____

When:

_____

_____

Where: _____

Complication
Events

- _____
- _____
- _____
- _____
- _____
- _____
- _____
- _____
- _____
- _____

Resolution

_____

_____

_____

_____

Snow White

Orientation
Characters:

_____

_____

_____

_____

What: _____

When:

_____

_____

Where: _____

Complication
Events

- _____
- _____
- _____
- _____
- _____
- _____
- _____
- _____
- _____
- _____

Resolution

_____

_____

_____

_____

Theme or main message of the story

Good will overcome evil

Orientation

Character/s	Description of Character/s
King Obah	Mean, rich and greedy
Arthur	Good, honest, poor hardworking, young man
Princess Eva	Unhappy daughter of King Obah
Wizard	Old and helpful to those who are good

Where: In the Kingdom of Obania

When: In the past

Complication
Events

- King Obah taxes his people heavily and gets rich by it.
- The King offers his daughter's hand to the man who proves to be the richest in the land.
- Arthur is in love with the Princess but he has little money.
- Arthur asks the Wizard to help.

Resolution
Wizard gives Arthur an invisible cloak. He slips into the castle and steals the King's riches and offers it to the King. The King is happy and agrees to let Arthur marry his daughter. After the wedding, Arthur shares his riches with all the people in the Kingdom.

There was once a rich King named Obah who was not well liked by his people. This was because he taxed them so much that they were all quite poor.

One day the King announced that he would offer his daughter's hand to the man who was the richest in the land. This announcement saddened Princess Eva because she knew that all the men in Obania were poor and she would have to live the rest of her life without a husband.

A young man named Arthur had been in love with Princess Eva for many years but, like the other townsfolk, he had little money. Arthur, however, was a clever, persistent young man. He went to visit the Wizard, an old, craggy man with a long, dirty white beard. There was a gleam in the Wizard's eyes when Arthur told him of his problem.

Reaching down, he picked up his withered old wand and waved it three times around Arthur. There before him was a silver cloak. The Wizard stated that it was an invisible cloak and that the person who wore it would not be seen. Arthur's eyes shone like lamps.

That night Arthur put on the cloak and crept into the King's castle. He crept down the long, winding corridor until he came to a room full of jewellery and coins. Arthur went back and forth a number of times, collecting riches on each trip. The King's guards were unaware of what had happened right under their noses.

The following day, Arthur returned to the castle and announced his intention to marry Princess Eva. King Obah laughed heartily but his jaw dropped when he saw Arthur's riches. Greedily, King Obah agreed to the wedding which took place that same day.

As the crowds turned out for the wedding, Arthur, who was now Prince Arthur, gathered his riches and threw it all out to the crowds. They threw their hats into the air and cheered. King Obah shrieked at the sight of all the riches being thrown away and he ran out of the castle, never to be seen again. Queen Eva happily ruled over the contented people.

Narrative Plan

After you have read the sample Narrative Plan on the facing page, use the plan below to help you write a narrative, making sure that each heading in the plan is covered.

Theme or main message of the story _____

Orientation

Character/s   Description of Character/s

_____   _____

_____   _____

_____   _____

_____   _____

Where: _____

When: _____

Complication Events

- _____
- _____
- _____
- _____

Resolution

_____

_____

_____

Write your short story based on the plan you have made.

_____

_____

_____

_____

_____

_____

_____

_____

_____

_____

_____

Read, discuss and study the word bank. Add some more theme words. Remember to LOOK, COVER, WRITE and CHECK when learning spelling.

wheelchair	hospital	overheard	doctor	condition
collapse	motionless	yesterday	moment	competition
helicopter	tomorrow	thought	paraplegic	quadriplegic
remember	question	answer	frustration	anger
although	sigh	relief	through	wonderful
tremble	allowed	stroke	blur	tumbling
_____	_____	_____	_____	_____
_____	_____	_____	_____	_____

Activity 1 - Group the list words into the categories below.

One syllable words (5) _____

Two syllable words (12) _____

_____

Three syllable words (9) _____

_____

Four syllable words (4) _____

Activity 2 - Write the thirty list words in dictionary order.

1._____ 2._____ 3._____ 4._____ 5._____

6._____ 7._____ 8._____ 9._____ 10._____

11._____ 12._____ 13._____ 14._____ 15._____

16._____ 17._____ 18._____ 19._____ 20._____

21._____ 22._____ 23._____ 24._____ 25._____

26._____ 27._____ 28._____ 29._____ 30._____

Activity 3 - WORD RULE

For adjectives that end in Y change the Y to I and add ER and EST, e.g. angry - angr*ier*-angr*iest*. Practise these.

a) lovely _____ _____   b) lonely _____ _____

c) merry _____ _____   d) weary _____ _____

e) happy _____ _____   f) healthy _____ _____

Activity 4 - FUN SPOT - SPELLING BINGO

Select nine words from the word bank and write them on the bingo grid. Play Spelling Bingo!

Read the text silently and complete activities on the following pages.

The Wheelchair

A lone tear rolled down the side of Vince's face as he lay in the hospital bed with its starched, white sheets. He had overheard his mother talking with the doctor about his condition.

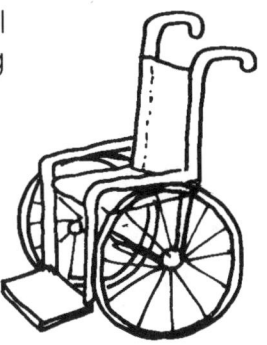

" I'm sorry...all we can do...not good...wait and see..."

"NO!...Oh no, no..." sobbed his mother.

Through the corner of one eye, Vince saw his mother collapse into a chair. He knew it would be bad news. His father, Bruno, sat motionless, his head in his hands.

Yesterday, everything was fine. The world was wonderful. In one fell swoop, in one awful moment, his world and that of his family, had come tumbling down.

Vince had been the star of the Murray Town Maulers football team. It was the last competition game before the semi-finals, when Vince had felt a crack in his neck while packing down in a scrum. He had collapsed in pain. What happened next was a blur. Voices. Yelling. Sirens. Helicopters.

The next thing Vince was aware of was the doctor speaking to his parents.

Bruno and Maria, his parents, came to his bedside. Maria stroked Vince's hair. Bruno, his voice trembling, said, "Nobody told us, Vince. You should never have been allowed to put your head in a scrum. Your neck is too long and thin."

For Vince, that night was the loneliest night he had ever spent. The nurses were nice, but he couldn't take his mind off the tests he was to have tomorrow. He thought of his parents and what they might be doing now. He thought of his team-mates who would be sitting at home watching football on TV. His mind was overflowing with thoughts.

Then there was the wheelchair by his bed. He wondered if he would have to sit in it for the rest of his life. He remembered a man in a wheelchair coming to his school to talk about paraplegics and quadriplegics. But he couldn't remember what the man had said.

His head was fighting a battle. He wanted to sleep, yet he feared that he might not ever wake up if he did. Questions filled his mind. He tried to answer them himself but he hoped that some of his answers would be wrong. Frustration and anger gave way to sleep.

Vince woke early to find himself being wheeled into a room for tests. He felt like a yo-yo, going back and forth for tests, scans and x-rays.

Finally, his parents came in, followed by the doctor.

"I'm afraid you will never play football again, Vince," stated the doctor, "but you will walk out of here in a few weeks. You are one lucky boy!"

Although sad, Vince knew how lucky he was. He was alive! He looked at the wheelchair and gave a sigh of relief.

✓

Answer the following questions in complete sentences after reading "The Wheelchair".

1. Why was Vince in hospital? _____

_____

2. How was Vince transported to hospital? _____

_____

3. What sport did Vince play? _____

4. How did Vince feel about what had happened ? Find two words in the passage
   that show how he felt. _____

_____

_____

5. What was the bad news that was given to Vince by the doctor? _____

_____

_____

6. What was the good news that was given to Vince by the doctor? _____

_____

_____

7. Why was Vince afraid to sleep? _____

_____

Vocabulary

1. Find a word from the story that means:

   a) fell down _____   b) not moving   _____

   c) shaking   _____   d) given permission _____

   e) strong feeling of annoyance _____

True or False?

1. Vince had been playing basketball.   _____

2. Vince felt a crack in his neck.   _____

3. An ambulance took Vince to hospital.   _____

4. Vince remembered a story about paraplegics and quadriplegics.   _____

5. Bruno is Vince's brother.   _____

6. It is safe for people with long, thin necks to pack into scrums.   _____

7. Vince had a number of tests the next morning.   _____

8. Vince felt lucky that he would be able to walk again.   _____

Circle the words that you think have been spelt incorrectly. Write the correct spelling for those words. There is one incorrect word for each line.

The pain that Vince felt was like a surge of electrisity

running all the way from his neck down to his spyne. He

fell to the ground, unabel to move.

1. _____

2. _____

3. _____

Vince heard a wistle blow and suddenly there was a

cluster of faces looking down at him. He squinted, triing

to focus on the players faceing him.

4. _____

5. _____

6. _____

He recernised the voice of his father, Bruno and the

coach, Brian. Thay were asking him how he was feeling.

At the same time he could hear players yelling. He cood

see the fear on their faces and he was sertain that

something terribel was wrong.

7. _____

8. _____

9. _____

10. _____

11. _____

Within minites, the monotonous whirring of helicopter

blades was herd.

12. _____

13. _____

A neck brayce was put around him and carefully, he was

lifted onto a strecher. The noise of the helicopter

became louder, and then he rememberd nothing.

14. _____

15. _____

16. _____

The next thing Vince remembered was walking up in

hospitle and hearing his mother talking to the doctor in a

frightened toan of voice.

17. _____

18. _____

19. _____

He had never been so

scarred in all his life !

20. _____

In "The Wheelchair", Vince is taken to hospital after being seriously injured during a football match. Do you think that football is a dangerous sport?

Write a discussion on this topic. Use the table below to plan your discussion, then write it out neatly on the facing page.

*Reasons why football **IS** a dangerous sport.*	*Reasons why football **IS NOT** a dangerous sport.*

Topic: Is Football a Dangerous Sport?

Introduction _____

_____

_____

_____

_____

Arguments _____

for and _____

against the _____

issue _____

_____

_____

_____

_____

_____

_____

_____

_____

_____

_____

_____

_____

_____

Recommendation _____

_____

_____

_____

The *setting* of a story describes where the important events in the story take place. Answer the questions below to find out more about the setting of "The Wheelchair".

The Wheelchair

In this space draw a picture of the setting.

Where did the story happen?

_____

_____

_____

_____

_____

Describe the place where the story happened.

_____

_____

_____

_____

_____

_____

_____

_____

_____

_____

_____

Does this story have more than one setting? Name some of these other places.

_____

_____

_____

Rewrite the following passage by correcting all spelling and adding punctuation.

no yelld vinces mother

she lookt ovur towards vince and colapsed into a chair

this cant be happening bruno sed he held his head in his hands

_____

_____

_____

Adverbs

Read these sentences and look carefully at the word underlined in each.

    a) <u>Gloomily,</u> Peter decided to go back home.

    b) She chained the bicycle <u>carefully</u> to the fence.

    c) Selina thought <u>suddenly</u> of the spa at the hotel.

The underlined words are called *adverbs*. They describe how something happens (they add information to verbs).

Rewrite the sentences below and change the underlined words into adverbs.

    1. "Can't you say my name <u>proper</u>?" asked Binh.

    _____

    2. Leila walked <u>slow</u> across the tiles of the bathroom.

    _____

    3. Rover ran <u>clumsy</u> towards his master.

    _____

    4. She turned <u>quick</u> as the door opened.

    _____

    5. Rajiv waited <u>hopeful</u> for Kelly's return.

    _____

Synonyms

Synonyms are words that have similar meanings, e.g. start - begin. Find a synonym for each of these words.

    a) difficult   _____   b) correct   _____

    c) quick   _____   d) little   _____

    e) repair   _____   f) lift   _____

Read, discuss and study the word bank. Add some more theme words. Remember to LOOK, COVER, WRITE and CHECK when learning spelling.

Earth	Mars	Saturn	Venus	Jupiter
Pluto	Mercury	Neptune	Uranus	planet
asteroid	meteor	comet	galaxy	Milky Way
· constellation	· astronomy	astronaut	orbit	· universe
shuttle	alien	intelligence	· observatory	telescope
solar	system	· eclipse	satellite	gravity
_____	_____	_____	_____	_____
_____	_____	_____	_____	_____

Activity 1 - *Syllables* In the table below categorise the list words into syllable groups.

One-syllable _____

Two-syllables _____

_____

_____

Three-syllables _____

_____

Four-syllables _____

_____

Activity 2 - *Smaller Words*

Find as many smaller words within the words listed below, e.g damage - dam, am, age.

1. Saturn _____
2. planet _____
3. satellite _____
4. telescope _____

Activity 3 - *Word Rule*

When a word ends in -Y and has consonants before it, change Y into I and add -LY, e.g. happy - happ*ily*. Practise these

1. angry _____   2. noisy _____   3. ready _____

4. steady _____   5. speedy _____   6. weary _____

7. wary _____   8. hasty _____   9. merry _____

Activity 4 - *Scrambled Words*

Unscramble each of the following list words.

1. tuloP _____   2. thuslet _____   3. brito _____

4. romeet _____   5. peslice _____   6. tragivy _____

7. steelpoce _____   8. austtaron _____   9. vineuser _____

10. liceingentle _____   11. octme _____   12. edirtsao _____

48

An alien has landed on Earth and you have been given the opportunity to ask **ten questions**. Think of questions that you can ask which will require a detailed response from the alien and write them below. ("How?" and "Why?" questions allow good responses!) Select a student in your class to play the part of the alien and have him/her answer the questions you have written. Think of some interesting answers to give!

Questions

1. _____

2. _____

3. _____

4. _____

5. _____

6. _____

7. _____

8. _____

9. _____

10. _____

Draw what you think the alien might look like.

Grammar - Joining Words

Who or That?

Join the following pairs of sentences by using one of the conjunctions above, whichever is more suitable.

1. I raced over to James.   He told me about the car accident.

_____

2. This is the new mystery novel.   I borrowed it from the Library.

_____

3. There is the horse.   It won the Melbourne Cup.

_____

4. I am the salesman.   I work in the Menswear Department.

_____

5. Melina is a girl.   She won a prize in the colouring-in competition.

_____

Writing a Narrative

Using the planning section below, create a narrative science fiction story. Think carefully about the types of characters found in science fiction before you choose them. Make sure that the narrative is set in the future.

Theme or main
message of the story   _____

Orientation

Character/s   Description of Character/s

_____   _____

_____   _____

_____   _____

_____   _____

Where   _____

When   _____

Complication

   Events

- _____

- _____

- _____

- _____

Resolution

_____

_____

From the plan you have developed, write the narrative in the space below.

Story Title _____

Orientation _____

(Who, when, _____

where?) _____

_____

_____

Events _____

_____

_____

_____

_____

_____

_____

Complication _____

_____

_____

_____

_____

_____

_____

Resolution

_____

_____

_____

_____

_____

_____

Select a planet in the solar system, complete the fact file and finish this design for a holiday brochure.

Visit our wonderful planet!

Our People

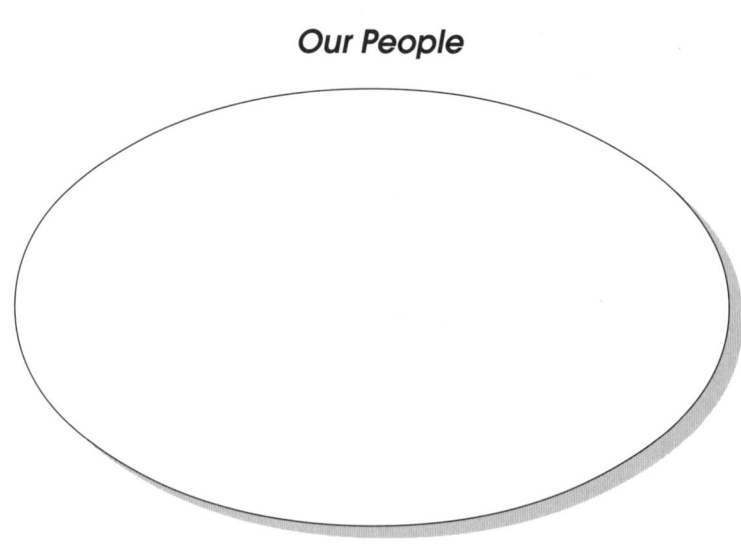

Fact File

Name of Planet _____

Distance from the Sun _____

Days taken to complete an orbit of the Sun

_____

Number of Moons _____

Name/s of Moons _____

_____

Size of Planet _____

Temperature _____

Description of its atmosphere _____

_____

What the planet is made of _____

_____

Special features _____

_____

Exploration on this planet _____

_____

_____

Sights to See!

_____

_____

_____

_____

Circle the words that you think have been spelt incorrectly. Write the correct spelling. There is one incorrect word for each line.

Aliens on the Moon?

It is clamed that two UFOs were watching as Neil

Armstrong took his first steps on the moon's surfice on July

20, 1969.

1. _____

2. _____

The astronaut spotted them on the edge of a crator as

he came out of the Apollo 11 spacecraft acording to a

top American space consultent.

3. _____

4. _____

5. _____

Wile Armstrong was contacting Houston to report the

sighting, his co-pilet, Buzz Aldrin filmed the alien craft from

Apollo 11.

6. _____

7. _____

However, NASA ordered that the incedent be covered

up. Staff at Mission Controll blacked out Armstrong's

report from broadcarsts all over the world.

8. _____

9. _____

10. _____

A Soviet space expert beleived that beings from another

civilisation picked up our radio signels and spied on the

mission to find out how knowledgable we where.

11. _____

12. _____

13. _____

There are other Amercan astronauts who have had close

encounters with straynge craft. In 1965, two astronauts, Ed

White and James McDivitt noticed a silver silinder with

antennae as thay

orbited Earth. They started to

take pictures but the object

moved toward them on a

colission course. The object

then misteriously vanished.

14. _____

15. _____

16. _____

17. _____

18. _____

19. _____

Rewrite the following passage using correct punctuation.

A man gary storey who was interested in UFOs claims to have exchanged messages with an unidentified object he set up a telescope on july 27 1967 to observe the moon but a bright light attracted his attention

storeys brother in law flashed a torch at the object three times and the object responded by flashing its light the same number of times after continuing to flash its lights the object vanished behind some trees

_____

_____

_____

_____

_____

_____

_____

_____

Confusing Verbs - Took or Taken?

Write the correct words. **I take   I took   I have taken**

1. I have _____ the books back to the Library.

2. Mai _____ a pen out of her bag.

3. We _____ a packed lunch with us.

4. A wallet was _____ from the house.

5. Have you _____ your keys with you?

Confusing Verbs - Spoke or Spoken?

Write the correct words. **I speak   I spoke   I have spoken**

1. I have _____ to the teacher.

2. Yesterday I _____ to the postman.

3. Carina _____ beautifully at the assembly.

4. A friend _____ calmly to the injured boy.

5. Have you _____ to your mother about it?

Mars is the fourth planet from the Sun. It is 228 million kilometres from the Sun and has two moons. A year on Mars is 687 days, while each day lasts for $24\frac{1}{2}$ hours.

Mars is a small planet, about half the diameter of the Earth and one tenth of its weight. It is often called the "red planet" because of the iron oxide or rust in its soil.

The planet is a desert with the exception of ice caps found at each end. On its dusty surface you will find boulders, huge extinct volcanos, giant canyons and what appear to be dried up river beds. Strong winds can blow up big storms of red dust. These make the sky look pink.

The atmosphere on Mars is thin and consists mainly of carbon dioxide. Occasionally, the surface temperature may rise slightly above 0°C. However the average temperature is -50°C and may drop to -135°C at the winter pole.

Many people believed that there may have been intelligent life on Mars. When two Viking spacecraft landed on Mars in 1976, an analysis of the soil showed no evidence of any kind of life. Recent reports in August 1996 told of a Martian meteorite found in Antarctica that contained signs of life. The Mars Pathfinder which landed on Mars on July 4th, 1997 may provide us with some clearer answers.

Comprehension
Answer all questions in full sentences.

1. Mars is what distance from the Sun? _____

_____

2. Why is Mars called the "red planet"? _____

_____

3. Describe the surface of Mars. _____

_____

4. What gas is mainly found in the atmosphere on Mars? _____

_____

5. Is there life on Mars? How do you know this? _____

_____

True or False?

1. A day on Mars is longer than a day on Earth. _____

2. Mars is heavier than the Earth. _____

3. You will find lots of water on Mars. _____

4. It is cold on Mars. _____

Read, discuss and study the word bank. Add some more theme words. Remember to LOOK, COVER, WRITE and CHECK when learning spelling.

newspaper international advertisement journalist attitudes language	report photograph articles business amuse comment	interview editorial columns finance entertain opinion	local cartoon headlines inform sensational event	national politics sport issues emotion world
_____	_____	_____	_____	_____
_____	_____	_____	_____	_____

Activity 1 - Word Meanings

Write a word from the list that means:

a) to make one laugh or smile _____

b) an important topic of discussion _____

c) the important news _____

d) a meeting where you ask questions _____

e) news around the country _____

Activity 2

Find smaller words within the words listed below, e.g. together - to, get, he, her.

a) journalist _____

b) newspaper _____

c) photograph _____

d) editorial _____

e) cartoon _____

Activity 3 - WORD RULE

When a word ends in a *silent E* drop the E add ING, e.g. shine - shining. Practise these.

a) measure _____   b) rescue _____   c) scribble _____

d) describe _____   e) amuse _____   f) excite _____

g) escape _____   h) bathe _____   i) please _____

Activity 4 - Making Words

Make as many words as you can from the grid below. You must use the central letter in all the words that you make.

r	t	e
i	**a**	c
m	s	p

_____ _____ _____ _____ _____

_____ _____ _____ _____ _____

_____ _____ _____ _____ _____

What is an Editorial?

Most newspapers have an editorial column where the Chief Editor puts forward a point of view for people to think about. This point of view is usually about current news issues that are of interest to the community.

The editor's opinions may differ from those of the reader and may spark some debate among readers. Sometimes the editorial can influence others to make a decision about the issue being discussed. It is important that we read an editorial and balance it with our own ideas about the topic before we make our own informed opinion.

It must be remembered that, unlike most other newspaper reports, which are fact, the editorial is an opinion. Its purpose is to help the readers to debate issues in the community.

An editor must be responsible and careful when selecting topics for his or her editorial as some topics may be very sensitive. The editor must also ensure that the opinion expressed is a strong one.

Comprehension

Answer all questions in full sentences.

1. What is the purpose of an editorial? _____

_____

2. Who writes the editorial? _____

_____

3. Why do you think editors should be careful about the topics that they write about?

_____

4. What sorts of things does an editor write about in editorials? Give examples. _____

_____

5. How can an editorial influence readers? _____

_____

True or False?

1. We should always have the same opinion as the editor.   _____

2. Editorials are generally about current news issues.   _____

3. The community is not interested in editorial articles.   _____

4. An editor must express strong opinions.   _____

5. Editorials give people something to think about.   _____

Many children's heroes are people who live in another country, e.g. American basketball stars. For some reason, few children have Australian heroes.

You are going to interview a famous Australian sportstar about heroes. After discussing the headings below, fill in the planning boxes to help you with your interview questions and then write your questions.

Names of Australian athletes that you believe are heroes	Qualities of these athletes that make them heroes	Why children should consider them to be heroes
1. _____	_____	_____
_____	_____	_____
_____	_____	_____
2. _____	_____	_____
_____	_____	_____
_____	_____	_____
3. _____	_____	_____
_____	_____	_____
_____	_____	_____
4. _____	_____	_____
_____	_____	_____
_____	_____	_____

Inverview Questions

1. _____
2. _____
3. _____
4. _____
5. _____
6. _____
7. _____

Writing an Editorial
After discussing why Australians need their own heroes, you are going to write an editorial about this topic on the next page. Remember that an editor must provide strong arguments to support his/her opinion. Make sure that you have discussed this issue thoroughly with your group.
The first column is for your rough copy but make sure that your second column is neat and tidy.

Write a draft editorial in the first column, then write the published copy in the second.
Remember to add the dates to your editorials.

Daily Mail

Date: _____

Australia needs its heroes!

_____
_____
_____
_____
_____
_____
_____
_____
_____
_____
_____
_____
_____
_____
_____
_____
_____
_____
_____
_____
_____
_____
_____
_____
_____

Daily Mail

Date: _____

Australia needs its heroes!

_____
_____
_____
_____
_____
_____
_____
_____
_____
_____
_____
_____
_____
_____
_____
_____
_____
_____
_____
_____
_____
_____
_____
_____
_____

When we write the actual words spoken by someone, we insert quotation marks. For example, "I really love going to the Easter Show," said Gary.

Rewrite the following sentences using quotation marks where necessary.

1. A passing motorist said the car just rammed straight into the pole.

   _____

2. The injured cricketer stated I expect to be back in training next season.

   _____

3. The blaze took control very quickly said the fireman.

   _____

4. The Prime Minister declared we will do all we can to help the needy.

   _____

5. What do you think caused the accident? asked the reporter.

   _____

Using Better Words

Rewrite the following sentences using better words for *get* or *gets*.

1. I need to get myself a new jumper.

   _____

2. I must admit I don't get what you are saying.

   _____

3. We have to get going soon.

   _____

4. Could you please get me a newspaper?

   _____

5. She gets a prize for winning the competition.

   _____

Past or Passed?

Passed means to go by, to do successfully, to send or hand to or to approve, e. g. She passed me a pen and a piece of paper.

Past means in time gone by, e.g. We have played netball in the past.

Complete the following sentences using either "past" or "passed".

1. I watched as the suspicious character _____ by my house.

2. The time is fifteen minutes _____ nine.

3. A law was _____ to outlaw the purchase of guns.

4. I _____ all of my exams at school.

5. As I walked _____ the old house, I noticed some shadowy movements.

Wizard Warne

Warne weaves web around Windies!

by David Hodges in Sydney

A magnificent display yesterday by Aussie spinner Shane Warne has tipped the scales in Australia's favour in the vital 5th Test in Sydney.

Despite an operation on his spinning finger in the off season, Warne, at times, spun the ball at right angles to capture 7-54 as the West Indies tumbled to be all out for 211.

It was a day when nothing seemed to go right for the Windies batsmen. First, there was an amazing run out when Brian Lara and Sherwin Campbell got involved in a mix-up, and then Lara swung wildly at a Warne delivery that rattled his off stump.

Warne was in superb form. He constantly fooled the Windies batsmen with a variety of deliveries from his bag of tricks.

He later said, "My spinning finger is as good as it's ever been. I was very happy with my form out there today. It certainly helps to have a good fielding side like we have".

Warne is now set to become the highest wicket-taking spinner in the history of the game provided he remains injury-free.

The Test continues today with Australia now in the box seat to take the series 3-2.

Comprehension

Answer all questions in full sentences.

1. Which team appears most likely to win the Test? _____

_____

2. Why is this team most likely to win the Test? _____

_____

3. What sort of bowler is Shane Warne? _____

_____

4. What was it that made Shane Warne's performance magnificent? _____

_____

5. How does Warne feel about his injury at the moment? _____

_____

True or False?

1. At the moment Australia leads the series by 3 Tests to 2. _____

2. Warne believes that the Australians are a good fielding side. _____

3. The West Indians were happy with their performance. _____

4. Shane Warne bowled Brian Lara. _____

5. Sherwin Campbell was run out. _____

61

Circle the words that you think have been spelt incorrectly. Write the correct spelling. There is one incorrect word on each line.

Three people were airlifted to hospital, one criticaley ill,

1. _____

after accedents in the Royal National Park yesterday.

2. _____

A man listed as critical at Sutherland Hospitel had

3. _____

suspected brain damige after bushwalking at Audley.

4. _____

The 39 year old man colapsed while walking with friends in

5. _____

steap bushland near Long Man's Leap at about 4:30 p.m.

6. _____

A Careflight spokesman said, "One of the group rased the

7. _____

alarm by contacting Emergancy Services on a mobile

8. _____

phone, and a medicel team was rushed in by helicopter to

9. _____

control his breatheing."

10. _____

While asisting the paramedics, two other members of the

11. _____

party slipped and badly spraned their ankles. They were

12. _____

also atended to and transported to Sutherland Hospital.

13. _____

Cloze Passage

Fill in the each blank with a word from the word bank.

last	shortly	residents	suffering
one	through	burnt	treated

A man lost all his possessions when a fire _____ down his house in North Sydney _____ night.

The fire ripped _____ his top-storey unit on Stringybark Road _____ after midnight.

North Sydney police said that all _____ from the five-storey block were evacuated and _____ elderly man was taken to hospital _____ from smoke inhalation.

A man was _____ for a cut to his arm and a woman received a cut to her head as they tried to escape.

Alliteration is a technique used by writers such as poets and editors to capture attention. It is when the writer repeatedly uses the same letter or sound to start two or more words in a group, e.g. Fierce flood flattens town!
Write sentences using alliteration to describe:

1. A warm day at the beach _____

2. A fire in a house _____

3. A car accident _____

4. A soccer player scoring a goal _____

5. An argument _____

Action Verbs

Action verbs are words that tell us what someone or something did, e.g. Brian rode his bike to the park.

Identify the action verbs in each sentence and list them.

1. The angry crowd spilled onto the playing field. _____

2. A runaway car crashed into a pole. _____

3. The desperate prisoner escaped from gaol. _____

4. A bystander rescued the injured child from the fire. _____

5. The fireworks lit up the sky. _____

Past, Present and Future Tense

The tense of a verb tells us when an action took place. For example,

The cow **jumps** over the moon.　　(**Present** Tense - it's happening now)
The cow **jumped** over the moon.　　(**Past** Tense - it has already happened)
The cow **will jump** over the moon.　　(**Future** Tense - it will happen in the future)

Rewrite the following sentences in the **past tense.**

1. The batsman scores a magnificent century.

_____

2. The Prime Minister introduces a law.

_____

3. The child plays games on a computer.

_____

4. The weary man mows the lawn.

_____

5. A lonely man finds a friend.

_____

Definition

An argument gives reasons why people have a certain opinion or point of view. They try to persuade others to agree with their opinion. e.g. Experiments on animals should be banned; Honesty is the best policy.

Features

Arguments/Expositions:

- are usually written in the present tense, but may change depending on the stage of the text.
- use joining words such as **because of, therefore, so, furthermore** when giving reasons.
- use other conjunctions to structure the argument, such as **firstly, also, secondly, finally.**
- use strong emotive words such as **I strongly believe, It is of great concern.**
- use a variety of verbs such as **running, hope, insist, shows, results in, indicates.**

Activities

Conjunctions/Joining Words

Use conjunctions to make two sentences become one.

1. The road was blocked.   We had to make a detour.

_____

2. The roof had a leak.   The carpet was soaking wet.

_____

3. I felt ill.   I decided to go to bed.

_____

4. Children should exercise regularly.   Some children are overweight.

_____

5. We should care for our waterways.   Marine life is dying.

_____

Strong emotive words.

Rewrite the following short argument by using strong emotive words instead of those underlined.

We <u>could</u> have heroes. I <u>think</u> they give us a role model to look up to. Kieren Perkins for example is a <u>good</u> example. It is <u>possible</u> that hard work made him achieve high standards.

_____

_____

_____

Dogs Make Better Pets Than Cats

It is known throughout the world that a dog is a man's best friend. Dogs make better pets than cats.

Thesis or Proposition

Point

Firstly, dogs are more friendly than cats. If you come home from school or work, you can be sure that your pet dog will be at the gate to greet you. Cats, it seems, may notice that you have arrived home, but they may not respond enthusiastically.

Elaboration

Argument

Point

Also dogs are happy to play games with people. They can often be seen catching balls or sticks and wrestling with their owners. If you're sad, your dog will always be there to comfort you.

Elaboration

Argument

Point

Some dogs also help to protect you and your home. If someone tries to break into your house while you are away, dogs may bark, and, in some cases, attack criminals. This protection could save the family a lot of time, money and heartache.

Elaboration

Argument

Point

Furthermore, dogs are more versatile. They help blind people to travel anywhere they like instead of just remaining at home. They have the ability to sniff out drugs and catch criminals in their capacity as police dogs. Cats do not do any of these things!

Elaboration

Argument

I believe that dogs make better pets and are more versatile than cats.

Conclusion

On a separate piece of paper, write an argument from a cat-lovers point of view.

Read, discuss and study the word bank. Add some more theme words. Remember to LOOK, COVER, WRITE and CHECK when learning spelling.

devastated	decide	bushranger	colonial	crime
terrify	violent	handkerchief	deliver	polite
moment	weather	roar	laugh	nervous
trooper	capture	protect	secretary	manager
through	billow	apologise	because	stagecoach
travel	vow	behave	shuffle	casual
_____	_____	_____	_____	_____
_____	_____	_____	_____	_____

Activity 1

Read the story on the opposite page then, choose words from the list to insert in the following sentences.

a) Bill's parents were _____ when they were kicked off their farm.

b) The Mild Colonial Boy covered his face with a purple _____.

c) A security guard managed to _____ Bill as he left the bank.

d) The bush people tried to _____ Bill because he gave them money.

e) Mrs Grimble was Mr Molloy's _____.

Activity 2

Build as many words as you can from the following. An example is given.

a) judge   judges, judged, judging, judgement

b) escape   _____

c) terrify   _____

d) behave   _____

e) deliver   _____

Activity 3

Find the meaning of the following words in the dictionary.

a) billow   _____

b) casual   _____

c) vow   _____

Activity 4 - FUN SPOT

Exploring Words. How many words can you make by joining any combination of the letters given? Write them below.

c	s	t	m	g	f	am	n	bl	e	d	r	ing

_____   _____   _____   _____   _____

_____   _____   _____   _____   _____

Read the text silently then, complete the activities on "The Mild Colonial Boy".

The Mild Colonial Boy

Many years ago, way in the outback, a little boy named Bill was born to a farmer and his wife. He was their pride and joy. As he grew up, he went to school and helped out on the farm when he came home. They were all very happy until one day some people from the bank came and kicked them off the land.

The farmer and his wife were devastated. They both became so ill that they died shortly after. Bill was sad and angry. He vowed to get even with all banks so he decided on a life of crime as a bushranger.

The problem with Bill was that he was so friendly and well-mannered. He didn't look or behave like a bushranger at all. Firstly, he shaved every day and did not look like the bearded bushrangers that people knew. Secondly, he wore glasses and finally, he always seemed to have a smile on his face. He never looked terrifying or violent. Bill always wore his hat down over his wide, blue eyes and a bright purple handkerchief covered his face.

One day, he hid behind a rock near a road. Moments later, a stagecoach came travelling across the bumpy, dirt road.

" Stand and deliver?" asked Bill politely.

The weatherbeaten, old stagecoach driver threw his head back and roared with laughter. Bill shuffled nervously, sneaked into the stagecoach, snatched the money bags and escaped into the bush. The driver was angry at his own stupidity, and he raced off to the nearest town to tell the troopers.

Before long, Bill was known as the "Mild Colonial Boy". Bill was very careful not to let the troopers capture him. The bush people loved him because of his shy nature and also because he gave much of his money to farmers who had been thrown off their land by the banks. For this reason, he was protected by the people. If ever troopers were near, Bill would have been warned. Before they could get anywhere near him, he would have been miles away.

Bill decided that he would rob the Middle Grove Bank. This was the bank that forced Bill's parents off their farm. Bill casually walked in and asked the secretary, Mrs Grimble, if he could see the Manager, Dan Molloy, about a loan. Mrs Grimble showed him into Mr Molloy's office.

Mr Molloy was a large, round man with little piggy eyes and a red face. He wore a grey suit that was a size too small so that his tummy stuck out of his trousers. In his mouth was a fat cigar through which clouds of smoke were billowing up into the misty room.

Mr Molloy swivelled in his chair and said, "So, how much are you after, Mr..."

"You may call me the Mild Colonial Boy," replied Bill, laughing. "I want it all!"

Quickly, he tied Mr Molloy to his chair, turned it around at a fast pace and grabbed the key to the safe. He apologised for the theft, said "good day" to Mrs Grimble and escaped on horseback.

Underline the words that you think have been spelt incorrectly. Write the correct spelling for each mistake in the table below.

The Mild Colonial Boy is the storey of a boy named Bill who is left all alone after his perents die. Bill is angry with the banks becuase one of them kicked his father and mother off there farm.

1. _____
2. _____
3. _____
4. _____

He gets the idea of becomeing a bushranger. First he decides to hold up the stagecoach. Even though he speeks in a polite way, he makes the stagecoach drivor look like a fool.

5. _____
6. _____
7. _____

On his advenchures, The Mild Colonial Boy robs the Middle Grove Bank. Mr Molloy, the bank manerger thinks that Bill is a customer. He is suprised when Bill tries to escape with all the money. Days later, security gard stops him and he is taken away by the troupers.

8. _____
9. _____
10. _____
11. _____
12. _____

In cort, Judge Martin is amazed because Bill blames the banks for his behaviour. An angrey Judge Martin sentences him to twentey-five years in Potter's Prison.

13. _____
14. _____
15. _____

Potter's Prison is a place where old bushrangers go to dye. However, The Mild Colonial Boy hatches a plan to exscape. He tells jokes to the prison offiser and makes him laugh so much that he drops his quays.

16. _____
17. _____
18. _____
19. _____

Quikly, Bill picks them up and hides them in his pocket. When darkness falls, he sneaks out of prison and creaps through the bush so that he cannot be herd.

20. _____
21. _____
22. _____

Write a headline and an accompanying newspaper report about the Mild Colonial Boy being captured at the Middle Grove Bank and being thrown in prison. In your report include the facts as they occurred. Your report must have the following characteristics:

- a catchy headline to capture attention
- date and place
- a lead sentence to encourage the reader to read on
- details: who, what, when why and how
- conclusion

Headline: _____

When we write the actual words that are spoken by characters we must enclose them in quotation marks. Rewrite the following sentences and insert speech marks and other punctuation where necessary.

1. Bill said i'm very lonely because i have no family and no friends

   _____

2. How much money would you like asked Mr Molloy

   _____

3. The Mild Colonial Boy stole my money gasped Mr Molloy

   _____

4. Stand and deliver called out the Mild Colonial Boy

   _____

5. Please come in replied Mrs Grimble

   _____

Contractions

Apostrophes are used in contractions where letters have been left out of a word,
   e.g. **was not** becomes **wasn't.**
Give the contracted form of the words in bold type.

1. **We will** go to the Middle Grove Bank at once.   _____

2. **Who is** that behind the handkerchief?   _____

3. **You are** going to gaol for robbing the bank.   _____

4. Please **do not** pour me any drinks.   _____

5. "But I **did not** steal your jewellery," replied Bill.   _____

Nouns, Verbs, Adverbs

For each noun listed add a verb to show action and add an adverb to show how that action was performed. The first one is done for you.

Noun	Verb	Adverb
cat	purred	happily
Mild Colonial Boy		
Mrs Grimble		
Mr Molloy		
the stagecoach driver		
dog		
clown		
athlete		

Imagine that you are a news reporter and you have been given an opportunity to interview some of the characters in "The Mild Colonial Boy". What questions would you ask? ("How?" and "Why?" questions allow good responses!) Think of questions that you can ask which will require a detailed response from each character and write them below. Then select some students in your class to play the parts of each character and have them answer the questions you have written. Think of some interesting answers to give!

Mild Colonial Boy

Interview Questions

1. _____
2. _____
3. _____
4. _____
5. _____

Old Stagecoach Driver

Interview Questions

1. _____
2. _____
3. _____
4. _____
5. _____

Dan Molloy

Interview Questions

1. _____
2. _____
3. _____
4. _____
5. _____

Mrs Grimble

Interview Questions

1. _____
2. _____

A Trooper

Interview Questions

1. _____
2. _____

Design a "Wanted" poster for "The Mild Colonial Boy" giving descriptions of physical appearance, character and what crimes / offences he has committed. Draw and colour in a picture of the character's face to illustrate your description.

WANTED

Name: _____

for _____

_____

_____

_____

_____

_____

_____

REWARD $_____

Carefully read the given cloze passage and use a better word for "said" in the blank spaces.

"Prisoner Bill," _____ Judge Martin with a snarl, "have

you anything to say before I sentence you?"

"Yes," _____ the Mild Colonial Boy.

"What?" _____ Judge Martin.

"Please don't send me to gaol, Your Honour," _____ The Mild Colonial Boy.

"It wasn't my fault, sir. Blame all the banks."

"You should have thought carefully before you chose to steal from stagecoaches

_____ the Judge.

"But I didn't hurt anyone," _____ The Mild Colonial Boy.

"You didn't?" _____ Judge Pepper angrily. "But you gave the

stagecoach driver a heart attack!"

"I'm sorry, Your Honour!" _____ The Mild Colonial Boy. "I didn't mean it."

Adverbs

Adverbs tell how, when, where or why things are done, e.g. walks **slowly**, looked
everywhere, worked **carefully.** Select adverbs from the box below to put into the story.

| fiercely | suspiciously | ferociously | carefully | sheepishly |

"I think you have my money," said Mr Molloy _____.

The security guard threw the purse over to Mr Molloy and he _____

counted his money. Then he looked _____ at The Mild Colonial Boy.

"There are some gold coins missing," he said.

The Mild Colonial Boy looked down _____. "Well maybe I did take them,"

he replied.

Mr Molloy's eyes narrowed as he stared _____ at Trooper O"Grady.

Homonyms

Underline the correct homonyms in brackets.

"Be (quiet, quite) my (deer, dear) bushranger," said Mr Molloy. Although he was
happy to (see, sea) The Mild Colonial Boy in prison, Mr Molloy wanted him taken to
(caught, court) straight away. (There, Their) was not a moment (two, too, to) (lose,
loose).

"I'm glad we have (caught, court) you," cried Mr Molloy, "I hope you will be (hear,
here) (for, four) ninety-nine years."

"Now (there, their) are plenty of jobs (for, four) you (two, too, to) do," replied Mr Molloy.

Read, discuss and study the word bank. Add some more theme words. Remember to LOOK, COVER, WRITE and CHECK when learning spelling.

gold	Australia	stole	attacked	bushranger
robbed	gang	colonial	coach	ballad
violence	accomplice	criminal	outlaw	pistol
weapon	murder	trooper	capture	reward
wanted	thief	gaol	hang	surround
hotel	shoot	infamous	notorious	kill
_____	_____	_____	_____	_____
_____	_____	_____	_____	_____

Activity 1

Find the meaning of the following words and then use each in a sentence.

a) accomplice   _____

_____

b) notorious   _____

_____

c) surround   _____

_____

Activity 2

Build on the given base words by adding the endings in the table (Watch your spelling!)

Base word	Add s	Add ed	Add ing	Suffix
rob	robs	robbed	robbing	robbery
murder	_____	_____	_____	_____
attack	_____	_____	_____	_____
surround	_____	_____	_____	_____
hang	_____	_____	_____	_____

Activity 3

Find complete words inside the ones given, e.g. palace - lace, pal.

gold _____	robbed _____	wanted _____
hotel _____	accomplice _____	trooper _____
infamous _____	outlaw _____	capture _____
bushranger _____	ballad _____	surround _____

Activity 4 - FUN SPOT

Make as many words as you can from the grid below. You must use the central letter in all the words that you make.

r	t	s
e	**a**	k
l	s	n

_____ _____ _____ _____

_____ _____ _____ _____

_____ _____ _____ _____

Choose the correct word from the brackets at the end of each sentence.

1. Mad Dog Morgan _____ some shocking things. (did, done)

2. The Tollkeeper _____ Captain Thunderbolt in a pub in town. (saw, seen)

3. Captain Moonlight and Captain Thunderbolt _____ just show-offs. (was, were)

4. The bushranger _____ away from the police. (rode, ridden)

5. Some bushrangers _____ poor people their money back. (gave, given)

Synonyms

Synonyms are words that have similar meanings, e.g friend - mate.
In the following set, one word does not belong to each group. Write out the three words that are similar in meaning.

1. large, big, right, huge   _____

2. leap, jump, hop, spring   _____

3. fast, run, speedy, quick   _____

4. hand, strange, odd, unusual   _____

5. smart, hid, clever, intelligent   _____

Antonyms

Antonyms are words that are opposite in meaning, e.g. friend - enemy.

Find the antonyms of the following words:

1. innocent _____

2. huge _____

3. straight _____

4. loose _____

5. rough _____

Adjectives

Adjectives are words that describe nouns, e.g. **tall, friendly** man. Replace the word "nice" with a better adjective.

1. a nice car _____

2. a nice picture _____

3. a nice dress _____

4. a nice movie _____

5. a nice teacher _____

Adverbs

An adverb tells us more about a verb, e.g. The bushranger rode **quickly.**

Add an adverb to the following sentences.

1. When the lady was robbed, she screamed _____.

2. The police searched _____ for the bushranger.

3. The happy bushrangers danced _____ at the hotel.

4. The lady sang _____ for the bushrangers.

5. Martin Cash escaped _____ from the prison.

Writing - Bushranger Report Planning sheet

Research and find detailed information on a bushranger of your choice using at least three sources of information. Carefully plan and draft your report before writing it on the page opposite. Make sure you cover the sub-headings listed.

a) Early life, e.g. date and place of birth, life as a boy

_____
_____
_____
_____

b) Other occupations

_____
_____
_____

c) Bushranging career, e.g. record of offences
d) Accomplices

_____
_____
_____
_____
_____
_____
_____
_____
_____

e) Death

_____
_____
_____

f) Bibliography - List of books/encyclopaedias etc and authors used.

_____
_____
_____

Bushranger Report on

_____

Opening
statement

_____
_____
_____

Early life,
(e.g. date
and place of
birth, life as a
boy/young
adult, other
occupations)

_____
_____
_____
_____
_____
_____
_____
_____
_____
_____

Bushranging
career (e.g.
details of
offences,
record of
offences,
accomplices
gaol
sentences,
and how
they died)

_____
_____
_____
_____
_____
_____
_____
_____
_____
_____
_____

Martin Cash

Early Life

Other Occupations

Martin Cash was born in County Wexford, Ireland in 1809. In 1828 he was sent to New South Wales for seven years for burglary. When he arrived, Cash was sent to work on a property in the Hunter Valley district. He worked so well that he quickly earned his ticket-of-leave, followed by a pardon.

Bessie Clifford, the wife of a former army officer was attracted to Cash and for many years she was known as "Mrs Cash". In 1837 there was trouble for Cash. He was accused of having stolen some cattle. Cash claimed that it was his partner who had committed the crime. However, Martin and Mrs Cash fled the colony, settling at Campbelltown in Tasmania (Van Diemen's Land). He quickly got into trouble, being charged with stealing farm produce and eggs. Consequently he was sentenced to seven years' hard labour. Cash escaped but was soon recaptured and given an additional two years on top of his sentence. The sentence was served at Port Arthur, near Hobart.

Bushranging Career and Accomplices

Here, he became friends with two bushrangers from NSW, George Jones and Lawrence Kavanagh. They offered to teach him the art of bushranging in return for his help to escape from the prison. The trio made their escape by swimming naked across an inlet, avoiding the guards and dogs. Stealing food and clothing from a nearby hut, they crept past a second line of guards and made their escape to the mainland.

They committed further robberies, being able to arm themselves and stock up on food. The trio built a fort of logs and earth for protection. Mrs Cash soon joined them here.

After more robberies, the colony panicked, and all available troops and police searched the bush with black trackers in an attempt to locate the outlaws. Determined to keep Mrs Cash safe, Martin Cash escorted the lady part of the way out of town, loaded up with stolen goods. However, she was arrested after she tried to sell some of these goods.

Cash held up a farm in Hamilton and sent a letter to the Governor, threatening to capture and flog him if Mrs Cash was not allowed to go free. The police released her, thinking that she may lead them to Cash's hideout. However, she sought refuge elsewhere and completely abandoned Cash, taking up with an ex-convict storekeeper, Thomas Pratt.

With Kavanagh wounded, Cash tried to take revenge on Mrs Cash and Pratt. He went to Hobart but the police were waiting. In the battle, one policeman was killed. Although sentenced to death, only Jones suffered that fate while Kavanagh and Cash were sent to Norfolk Island for life.

Death

Cash returned to Tasmania with his wife, a convict woman servant, in 1854 after being given a ticket-of-leave. He was made caretaker of the Government Gardens and later went to New Zealand. Cash returned to Hobart four years later after buying an orchard in Glenorchy. After writing his memoirs, Martin Cash died in 1878. He is one of only two bushrangers not to die a violent death.

From the report on the bushranger, Martin Cash, answer the following questions in full sentences.

1. Why was Martin Cash sent to NSW? _____

   _____

2. Why did Martin Cash leave the NSW colony to settle in Campbelltown, Tasmania?

   _____

   _____

3. For what crime was Cash sentenced to seven years' hard labour? _____

   _____

4. Why did Cash have to serve two extra years on top of his sentence? _____

   _____

5. Where did Cash meet the two bushrangers from NSW? _____

   _____

6. How did Martin Cash, George Jones and Lawrence Kavanagh escape from prison?

   _____

   _____

7. Why was Mrs Cash arrested? _____

   _____

8. Why did Cash want to take revenge on Mrs Cash and Thomas Pratt? _____

   _____

Timeline

Using the report on Martin Cash, construct a timeline using the table below.

Year	Event/s
1809	• _____
1828	• _____
1837	• _____
1837-1854	• _____
	• _____
	• _____
	• _____
	• _____
	• _____
	• _____
1854	• _____
1878	• _____

Spelling - Proofreading

Circle the words that you think have been spelt incorrectly. Write the correct spelling for each mispelt word.

When the Kelly gang went to Jerilderie, in New South Whales they held up the police stashen and locked the officers in a jail. The gang escorted evryone into the pub where they gave them drinks. Then they robed the bank with Ned Kelly burning all the morgage papers as he didn't want the farmers to oh money to the bank.

1. _____
2. _____
3. _____
4. _____
5. _____
6. _____

The police tried desprately to capture Mad Dog Morgan. He had shot a police sergeant in cold blud after the sergeant had bidden him good mawning.
Morgan was shot dead arfter holding up Peechelba Station. A servant girl had exscaped and raised the alarm.

1. _____
2. _____
3. _____
4. _____
5. _____

Cloze Passage

Complete the cloze passage using words from the word bank.

instead	house	bushranger	husband's	people
who	Bathurst	occasion	life	because

Ben Hall was an unusual bushranger _____ he didn't like the idea of killing _____. In fact, at least on one _____, he stepped in to save the _____ of a victim.

When Hall's gang attacked Commissioner Keightley's _____, the Commissioner had returned fire, killing a _____ named Burke. This angered Burke's mate, John Vane _____ wanted to kill Keightley. However, Hall intervened and _____ got Mrs Keightley to travel to _____ to raise a ransom in return for her _____ life.

Capitals are used:
- at the beginning of sentences
- for subject headings
- for proper nouns
- for important words in titles

Rewrite the following sentences using capital letters where required.

1. john donahoe was born in dublin in 1806.

   _____

2. captain melville spent christmas in geelong.

   _____

3. frank gardiner was sent to the prison on cockatoo island.

   _____

4. the kelly gang were camped at stringybark creek.

   _____

5. john caesar arrived in new south wales in march 1789.

   _____

Collective Nouns

Collective nouns are names given to groups of similar objects. e.g a **herd** of cattle, a **crowd** of people. Match the collective nouns in the box to the phrases given.

litter	fleet	army	choir	school	cluster	board	swarm

1. An _____ of soldiers
2. A _____ of stars
3. A _____ of pups
4. A _____ of directors
5. A _____ of whales
6. A _____ of singers
7. A _____ of ships
8. A _____ of bees

The Comma

Commas can indicate where a reader should pause, and they can be used to separate parts of sentences, e.g. Fred Ward, a bushranger, was born in 1836.

Rewrite the following sentences and add commas.

1. Michael Howe a sailor became a highwayman.

   _____

2. Ned Kelly a hero to many was executed in 1880.

   _____

3. Johnny Dunn a former jockey joined Ben Hall's gang.

   _____

4. Morgan a cold-blooded killer was shot by Paddy Quinlan.

   _____

Read, discuss and study the word bank. Add some more theme words. Remember to LOOK, COVER, WRITE and CHECK when learning spelling.

endanger	Australia	species	habitat	environment
clear	introduce	chemical	pesticide	predator
breed	survive	marsupial	capture	extinct
hunt	destroy	forest	grassland	mountain
conserve	compete	protect	rare	swamp
threat	carnivore	herbivore	omnivore	native
_____	_____	_____	_____	_____
_____	_____	_____	_____	_____

Activity 1
Build on the given base words by adding endings in the table (watch your spelling!)
An example has been given.

Base word

destroy	destroys	destroyed	destroying	destruction
introduce	_____	_____	_____	_____
conserve	_____	_____	_____	_____
protect	_____	_____	_____	_____
survive	_____	_____	_____	_____

Activity 2 - Word Rule:
For words ending in a short vowel followed by a single consonant, **double the last consonant** before adding **-er, -ed** and **-ing**. Not all will have an **-er** ending, e.g. slam - slammer, slammed, slamming. Practise the following.

1. occur _____
2. slip _____
3. plan _____

Activity 3
Find complete words inside the ones given e.g. palace - lace, pal.

clear	_____	forest	_____	capture	_____
breed	_____	herbivore	_____	rare	_____
threat	_____	habitat	_____	mountain	_____
compete	_____	pesticide	_____	swamp	_____

Activity 4 - FUN SPOT
Make as many words as you can from the grid below. You must use the central letter in all the words that you make.

l m r   _____ _____ _____ _____ _____

e **i** k   _____ _____ _____ _____ _____

s t o   _____ _____ _____ _____ _____

Fact File: The Numbat

The Numbat is one of the most beautifully coloured marsupials. It is a reddish-brown colour with markings across the rump and a black stripe across each side of its eyes.

It was once found in southern parts of Australia but can now only be found in a small part of Western Australia. They live in eucalypt forests, sheltering in low scrub and hollow logs.

Numbats are diurnal animals. This means that they sleep at night and are awake during the day.

Numbats like to dig into rotten logs where they find termites, their main source of food. They use their long, sticky, worm-like tongues to lick up these termites and ants.

Numbats do not have pouches so when the young are born, they attach themselves to teats and cling to the fur of the mother's belly. The mother will sometimes dig a burrow with a nest at the end to protect her young.

This animal is endangered because forests are being cleared. Therefore their habitat is being destroyed. Numbats are also hunted and killed by foxes.

After reading the Fact File, complete the information about the Numbat in the boxes below.

Description	*Food*	*Habitat*
_____	_____	_____
_____	_____	_____
_____	_____	_____
_____	_____	_____
_____	_____	_____
_____	_____	_____

Babies

_____
_____
_____
_____
_____
_____

Why this animal is endangered

_____
_____
_____
_____
_____
_____

Numbat

Pronouns are words used in place of a noun to avoid that noun being repeated. For example, without the pronouns "he" and "him", we would have to write:

> Thanh told David that David could come to the movies with Thanh.

A better sentence is:

> Thanh told David that he could come to the movies with him.

Underline the correct pronouns in brackets in the following passage.

Baw Baw frogs live high on Mt Baw Baw in Victoria. (They, It) are becoming endangered because Mt Baw Baw has been developed as a ski resort. (His, Their) habitat has been destroyed. (They, It) tend to live near water under rocks and logs. (You, I) may find small warts on (him, them).

Conjunctions

Conjunctions are words that join single words or group words. Examples of conjunctions:

because	since	that	and	unless	though	for	but
whether	until	when	while	yet	although	if	as

Join each pair of sentences, using the conjunction in brackets.

1. There were many woodhens.   They had no natural predators.   (because)

   _____

2. Northern hairy-nosed wombats eat grasses.   They eat other vegetation. (and)

   _____

3. Numbats sleep at night.   Numbats are awake by day.   (and)

   _____

4. Leadbeater's possum was believed to be extinct.   They were re-discovered in 1961. (but)

   _____

5. Ghost bats are endangered. Mining has destroyed their habitats.   (because)

   _____

Antonyms and Synonyms

Find an antonym (opposite) and a synonym (word of similar meaning) for each word.

Word	Antonym	Synonym
quiet		
quick		
coarse		
help		
easy		

Research and find detailed information on an Australian endangered animal of your choice, using at least three sources of information. Carefully plan and draft your report before writing it below. Make sure you cover the sub-headings listed.

Endangered Animal Report on

_____

Opening
statement

_____
_____
_____

Facts about
the topic,
e.g. Why the
animal is
endangered.

_____
_____
_____
_____
_____
_____
_____
_____

Strategies
being used
to save the
animal from
extinction

_____
_____
_____
_____
_____
_____
_____
_____
_____

More Facts

_____
_____

The possible
future of
this animal

_____
_____
_____

Circle the words that you think have been spelt incorrectly. Write the correct spelling for each mispelt word.

The Ghost bat has pale gray fur, a hairless nose and large
ears. The only carnivorous bats in Austraila, they live in the
north, in groups called colonies. They are nocternal, resting in
caves or mines during the day and hunting at nite.

1. _____
2. _____
3. _____
4. _____

They eat small animals such as frogs, birds, lizerds and mice.
They swoop upon their prey and wrap it in their wings befor
biting and kiling it.

5. _____
6. _____
7. _____

Ghost bats have become endangered because mineing
operations are threatening to distroy their habitat

8. _____
9. _____

Comprehension

Answer the following questions about the proofreading passage above.

1. What is unique about this type of bat in Australia? _____

_____

2. In what part of Australia will you find Ghost bats? _____

_____

3. Why is the Ghost bat beginning to die out? _____

_____

4. Write the sentence that proves that Ghost bats are carnivorous. _____

_____

5. What is the Ghost bats' habitat? _____

_____

True or False?

1. Ghost bats sleep at night.   _____
2. Ghost bats only eat plants.   _____
3. Ghost bats rest in dark places.   _____
4. Large animals are endangering Ghost bats.   _____
5. Other bats in Australia are carnivorous.

Commas can be used to separate nouns that are close together. This is called "nouns in apposition", e.g **Kenny, the koala,** climbed the tree; I gave an ice cream to **Branko, my best friend**.

Rewrite the following sentences and insert commas where necessary.

1. The Nabarlek a kind of wallaby usually grazes at night.

_____

2. The Platypus a marsupial sleeps for most of the day.

_____

3. Our favourite animal the Koala eats only eucalyptus leaves.

_____

4. A nocturnal animal the Kowari hunts large insects and mice.

_____

5. Like the Cuscus the Striped possum lives alone.

_____

Punctuation

Punctuate the following passage by rewriting it below.

Like all cockatoos pink cockatoos have strong beaks which they use to crack seeds and nuts they feed on the seeds of grasses and the fruits of trees like wattles cypresspines and she-oaks you will find them in the dry centre of australia although they have been found near the coast in victoria and south australia

_____

_____

_____

_____

_____

Went or Gone?

1. She has now _____.

2. Linh _____ shopping after school.

3. They have _____ to New Zealand for two weeks.

4. Do you know Carlos _____?

Discuss the following statement in your group:

Should Zoos play a part in the survival of endangered species of animals?

• Your group members may either agree or disagree with this statement but they must give reasons for thinking the way they do.

• List reasons from both viewpoints below and be prepared to discuss the statement with the whole class. Write a discussion on the next page.

Reasons why Zoos should play a part in the survival of endangered species of animals.

_____

_____

_____

_____

_____

_____

_____

_____

_____

_____

_____

_____

_____

_____

_____

_____

_____

_____

_____

_____

_____

_____

Reasons why Zoos should NOT play a part in the survival of endangered species of animals.

_____

_____

_____

_____

_____

_____

_____

_____

_____

_____

_____

_____

_____

_____

_____

_____

_____

_____

_____

_____

_____

_____

Topic: **Should Zoos play a part in the survival of endangered species of animals?**

Introduction _____
_____
_____
_____

One point
of view _____
_____
_____
_____
_____
_____
_____

Other point
of view _____
_____
_____
_____
_____
_____
_____

Conclusion
Your opinion _____
_____
_____
_____
_____

Text Type - Information Report

Definition

An Information Report supports, stores, organises and presents information accurately. Only the important facts are written and put together in an organised way. See the report on spiders opposite.

Features

Reports:
- use nouns, e.g earthquakes, spiders.
- use some action verbs particularly when describing behaviour.
- use relational verbs (linking words such as are, have, belongs to).
- are usually in the present tense.
- sometimes use scientific or technical terms.

Present Tense

Change the following sentences to present tense.

1. There were over 3 000 species of spiders.

_____

2. The spider's silk was strong and elastic.

_____

3. Spiders produced silk from glands in the abdomen.

_____

4. A spider crushed the hard parts of its victims body.

_____

5. Some spiders performed courtship dances.

_____

Relational Verbs

Add one of the following relational verbs to the following sentences.

are	have	has	belong to

1. A spider _____ eight legs.

2. Spiders _____ related to scorpions.

3. Female spiders _____ able to lay large numbers of tiny eggs.

4. Spiders _____ the ability to spin silk.

5. Spiders _____ the group called arachnids.

6. Spiders _____ little sense of hearing and smell.

<table>
<tr><td></td><td>There are over 3000 species of spiders and they belong to the Arachnid family.</td><td>*General Classification*</td></tr>
</table>

Appearance

Spiders are not insects, but are related to scorpions and other arachnids that have eight legs and no antennae.

Most spiders have poor eyesight and little sense of hearing and smell. They do, however, have a well developed sense of touch in the hairs and spines that cover their body

They may vary in size from about 1mm to a giant 200 mm.

Description

Behaviour

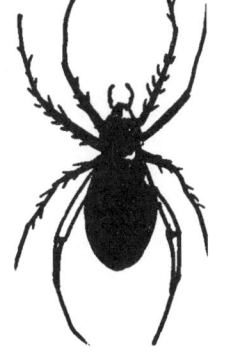

Spiders are well known for their ability to spin silk. They are able to produce this from glands in the abdomen and the silk comes out through organs called spinnerets.

The silk is strong and elastic and is used to trap the spider's prey. Spiders use their webs in different ways. Some weave a net to throw over their prey, while others attach a sticky blob to the end of a silken thread and whirl it around in a circle to wrap around an insect.

Description

Food

Spiders suck the fluids from their victims rather than eat solid food. Then they crush the hard parts, mixing them with digestive juices to make them into a liquid as well.

Description

Reproduction

Female spiders lay large numbers of tiny eggs and cover them in a silken sac. Some species carry this sac around with them. When first hatched, the young resemble adults and slowly develop to full size.

Before mating, some spiders perform courtship dances. After mating, some male spiders are eaten by the female.

Description

On a separate piece of paper write a report on the Funnel Web or Redback spider.

Read, discuss and study the word bank. Add some more theme words. Remember to LOOK, COVER, WRITE and CHECK when learning spelling.

heart	circulatory	blood	ligament	atrium
ventricle	artery	aorta	oxygen	cardiac
muscle	respiratory	digestive	skeletal	nerve
vertebra	retina	pupil	lens	canal
cochlea	eardrum	stomach	throat	intestine
liver	pancreas	kidney	collarbone	cartilage
_____	_____	_____	_____	_____
_____	_____	_____	_____	_____

Activity 1

Find the meaning of the following words in the dictionary and use each in a sentence.

a) cardiac _____

_____

b) cartilage _____

_____

c) retina _____

_____

Activity 2

Find smaller words inside the words listed below. e.g. intestine - in, test, tin.

a) collarbone _____
b) heart _____
c) cartilage _____
d) eardrum _____

Activity 3 - WORD RULE

For many of the words ending in F and FE, change the F or FE to V and add -ES
e.g knife - knives.   Practise these:

a) belief _____   b) life _____   c) wife _____

d) thief _____   e) half _____   f) shelf _____

g) grief _____   h) wolf _____   i) calf _____

Activity 4 - FUN SPOT - MAGIC WORDS

Change **MATE**   **SHIP**
         into   into
         KIND   **BLOW**

The rules are:
- Change one letter at a time.
- Make a real word each time you change a letter.
- You may change the order of the letters.
- Use block letters.

e.g.	MATE	CAST	MINT
	MANE	_____	_____
	MINE	_____	_____
	MIND	_____	_____
	KIND	WORD	DATE

The word **or** is used when we wish to make a choice.
For example, you may have ham **or** cheese on your sandwich.

The words **before, after, until, when, while** are conjunctions of time.
They are used to show when something happens.
For example, you cannot watch TV **until** your homework is completed.

Rewrite the following pairs of sentences by using one of the joining words above, whichever is most suitable, to make one sentence.

1. I will do the dishes.   You dry the dishes.

_____

2. Go soon.   The shops may close.

_____

3. He will give me the money.   I will see him tomorrow.

_____

4. You should brush your teeth.   Go to school.

_____

5. You may not have dessert.   Finish your dinner.

_____

Using Correct Punctuation

Rewrite the following passage using correct punctuation.

the human body is made up of a number of systems it is an amazing machine some of the systems include the circulatory the nervous and the skeletal systems we should make sure that we look after our bodies this will keep us healthy

_____

_____

_____

_____

Synonyms and Antonyms

Find a synonym and an antonym for each of the following words.

Word	Synonym	Antonym
miserable		
defeat		
high		
complete		
leave		

Blood is a red, sticky substance that carries food and oxygen around the body through arteries and veins. It is made up of four things: plasma, red blood cells, platelets and white blood cells.

Plasma is a yellowish, watery fluid containing millions of different cells that take proteins, chemicals, food and wastes around the body.

Red blood cells carry oxygen around the body.

White blood cells eat up germs and other rubbish that may enter the body. Basically, the purpose of white blood cells is to fight and destroy bacteria.

Blood platelets help to heal injuries that we get when we lose blood. They stick to the walls of blood vessels where an injury has occurred and they help to form a clot, the first step in the healing of an injury. Clotting stops us from losing too much blood.

Blood flows through tubes known as blood vessels. The larger vessels are called arteries and veins. Smaller blood vessels are called capillaries.

There are four main blood groups - A, B, AB and O. It is important that people know which blood group they belong to because if people have blood transfusions with blood from the wrong group, the red cells will clump together. Severe reactions may occur or even death.

Comprehension

Answer all questions in full sentences.

1. What is blood made up of? _____

_____

2. What does plasma do? _____

_____

3. What is the purpose of white blood cells? _____

_____

4. Name the different types of blood vessels. _____

_____

5. What could happen if you were given a transfusion from the wrong blood group?

_____

_____

True or False?

1. Platelets form clots to help heal injuries.   _____

2. Veins are smaller than capillaries.   _____

3. Red blood cells carry oxygen.   _____

4. It is okay to be given a transfusion of any blood type.   _____

94

Circle the words that you think have been spelt incorrectly. Write the correct spelling for each mistake. There is one incorrect word on each line.

The skeleton concists of over two hundred bones. It gives
our body shape and enabels us to move. The skeleton also
helps to protect importent organs such as the brain, the
hart and the lungs.

1. _____
2. _____
3. _____
4. _____

To ensure movement, we have bones, musles and joints.
Joints are wear two bones meet. Some examples are
sholders, knees, elbows and wrists.

5. _____
6. _____
7. _____

Some moveable joints are called hinge joints becuase they
only allow movement in one direcsion. Examples are
elbows, knees, tows and fingers.

8. _____
9. _____
10. _____

All bones have speshal names. The skull is called the
cranium and the backbone is called the spinal colum.

11. _____
12. _____

The bones of an adult are very hard and britle while babies'
bones are soft. As children grow, there bones harden.

13. _____
14. _____

When a bone is fractored, you will be unable to use the
injured part. Their will also be pain and swelling.

15. _____
16. _____

You should not touch the injery because you may do
further damage to it. Insted, use ice packs to reduce pain
and swelling and get medicel help.

17. _____
18. _____
19. _____

True or False?

1. Hinge joints move in many directions.   _____

2. The cranium helps to protect the brain.   _____

3. An elbow is a joint.   _____

4. You should move a child's arm to see if it's broken.   _____

5. Ice packs help reduce the swelling of an injury.   _____

Apostrophes may be used to show that a letter or letters have been left out.

isn't - is not   the "o" has been left out and is replaced by the apostrophe.

I'll - I will   the "w" and "i" have been left out and are replaced by the apostrophe.

Write the shortened form of the following:

1. you are _____
2. was not _____
3. I have _____

4. we will _____
5. I would _____
6. she is _____

7. cannot _____
8. they are _____
9. here is _____

Write these contractions in full.

1. couldn't_____
2. haven't _____
3. she'll _____

4. mustn't _____
5. you're _____
6. he'd _____

Good or Well?

Good is an adjective (describing word), for example, She is a good player.

Well is an adverb (adds meaning to a verb), for example, She is playing well.

Use **good** or **well** in these sentences.

1. Our doctor said that my heart was recovering _____.

2. I was breathing _____ after the cross-country run.

3. Lucia had a _____ day at the park.

4. My skin is _____.

5. The blood was not pumping _____.

Wrote or Written?

1. Lily has _____ a lovely letter to her pen-pal.

2. He _____ his report and gave it to his teacher.

3. Have you _____ your poem into your book?

4. Mohammed _____ neatly in his book.

5. The animal report was well _____.

There, Their or They're?

1. _____ going to the zoo tomorrow.

2. They brought _____ books to school.

3. _____ are over two hundred bones in a skeleton.

4. Are _____ any biscuits left?

5. _____ buying _____ movie tickets today.

When we eat food, it must be digested before the body can use it for growth and energy. Digestive juice joins with the food at various times. The process of digestion commences in the mouth and continues as the food passes down through the digestive tract.

When we start eating, the food is chewed and mixed with our saliva. This softens it, making it easier for our tongues to roll it into a ball and enable the food to be swallowed. After this, the food is pushed through the oesophagus into the stomach.

Here, the food is churned and mixed with digestive juices and acid. The food remains in the stomach for one to four hours.

The mixture then moves on to the intestines where it is slowly pushed through. While this is happening, food that can be used by the body is gradually absorbed. Wastes that the body does not require are removed through the anus.

Sometimes our stomachs get upset. When this happens we should not have food but drink plenty of fluids.

Comprehension

Answer all questions in full sentences.

1. What must be done to the food before it can be used for growth and energy?

   _____

2. How does our saliva help us to digest food? _____

   _____

3. Where does the food pass before it gets to the stomach? _____

   _____

4. What happens to the food in the stomach? _____

   _____

5. How do the intestines help in the digestive system? _____

   _____

True or False?

1. Waste from the body goes out through the anus. _____

2. Food may stay in the stomach for three hours. _____

3. Acid mixes with the food in the stomach. _____

4. Digestion stops when food enters the intestines. _____

5. More saliva mixes with food in the stomach. _____

Science Experiment - Bones

Investigate to find out how bones react when placed in vinegar for a week.

- Bring in some cleaned chicken bones and a glass jar with a lid.

- Place the bones into the jar with the vinegar. (Make sure the vinegar covers the bones completely.)

- Discuss with your group what happens after a week has elapsed.

In this space predict what you think might happen and why it might happen.

_____

_____

_____

_____

_____

On the next page is space to write up your experiment.

- The Aim of your experiment should tell what you were trying to find out by doing the experiment.

- The Equipment section is where you list all the equipment you used for this experiment.

- The Procedure section should list in order all the things you did during the experiment.

- The Results section is where you write down your observations (i.e. what happened).

- The Conclusion is where you answer your aim, (i.e. from the experiment, what did you find out?).

Draw your results from the experiment in this box.

Experiment - Bones

Aim: _____
_____
_____

Equipment: _____
_____
_____

Procedure:

1. _____
2. _____
3. _____
4. _____
5. _____
6. _____
7. _____
8. _____
9. _____
10. _____

Results: _____
_____
_____
_____
_____
_____
_____

Conclusion: _____
_____
_____
_____

Read, discuss and study the word bank. Add some more theme words. Remember to LOOK, COVER, WRITE and CHECK when learning spelling.

hunger	appetite	nutrition	thirst	fluid
benefit	substance	health	vegetables	survive
sweat	weight	energy	growth	strength
carbohydrate	protein	digest	dairy	calcium
vitamins	minerals	balance	fibre	sugar
important	breakfast	ingredient	lethargic	restless
_____	_____	_____	_____	_____
_____	_____	_____	_____	_____

Activity 1

Match the meaning with its word.

a) the wish for food and drink

b) to break down in your stomach and intestines

c) the state of being lazy

d) to give out a salty liquid through the skin

e) soft silver-white metal found in teeth and bones

f) the part of food that can't be digested

digest

sweat

calcium

appetite

fibre

lethargic

Activity 2

Place the given list words in dictionary order

1._____ 2._____ 3._____ 4._____ 5._____

6._____ 7._____ 8._____ 9._____ 10._____

11._____ 12._____ 13._____ 14._____ 15._____

16._____ 17._____ 18._____ 19._____ 20._____

21._____ 22._____ 23._____ 24._____ 25._____

26._____ 27._____ 28._____ 29._____ 30._____

Activity 3 - WORD RULE

For nouns that end in O coming after a vowel (A, E, I, O, U) add -S to make them plural.
e.g. piano - pianos Practise these:

a) silo _____   b) radio _____   c) studio _____

d) zero _____   e) banjo _____   f) soprano _____

g) solo _____   h) rodeo _____   i) merino _____

Activity 4 - FUN SPOT

Can you turn the following words into shapes?

SIZZLE   FLY   BREAK

Be prepared to debate an important issue in your classroom. A member of your class believes that children eat too much junk food. What do you think of this? In the table below, list reasons for and against the statement and then debate it in class.

Yes! Children eat too much junk food.

1. _____
   _____
   _____
   _____

2. _____
   _____
   _____
   _____

3. _____
   _____
   _____
   _____

4. _____
   _____
   _____
   _____

5. _____
   _____
   _____
   _____

6. _____
   _____
   _____
   _____

No! Children do not eat too much junk food.

1. _____
   _____
   _____
   _____

2. _____
   _____
   _____
   _____

3. _____
   _____
   _____
   _____

4. _____
   _____
   _____
   _____

5. _____
   _____
   _____
   _____

6. _____
   _____

Two words that are often used to join sentences are **and** and **but**.

The word **and** is used to give additional information to a sentence, e.g. I like ham and cheese on my sandwich.

The word **but** is used when something unexpected happens. e.g. I like ham but I don't like cheese.

Rewrite the following pairs of sentences as one by using either **and** or **but**.

1. I like to drink milk.   I like to drink fruit juice.

_____

2. Coffee contains caffeine.   Cola contains a dangerous drug called caffeine.

_____

3. A little salt is okay.   Too much salt increases your blood pressure.

_____

4. We tried to improve his diet. He would not follow the diet.

_____

5. Milk contains calcium.   Cheese contains calcium for strong bones and teeth.

_____

Prefixes

A prefix is a word part put in front of words to change the meaning or form new words. The prefix RE usually means to **go back** or **do again**, e.g. call - recall.

Add the prefix RE to the following words.

1. arrange _____   2. count _____   3. fresh _____

4. cycle _____   5. play _____   6. gain _____

7. create _____   8. cover _____   9. heat _____

The prefix **PRE** usually means something that is done beforehand, e.g. preview - showing of a film **before** the public has seen it.

Find the meanings of the following **PRE**- words.

1. prepare   _____

2. prelude   _____

3. predict   _____

4. precede   _____

5. precaution   _____

Use **two** of the above **PRE** words in sentences to show their meanings.

1. _____

2. _____

Circle the words that you think have been spelt incorrectly. Write the correct spelling for each mispelt word. There is one incorrect word on each line.

Most eggs that are eatin in the world are eggs that come from chickens. Chickens are rased in most countries because they can cope with most types of climete.

1. _____

2. _____

3. _____

Chickens are kept in types of cages called battries. When an egg is layed, it rolls down a ramp out of the cage and onto a conveyer belt. The eggs are then takin to a packing room and placed into cartens. In some countries eggs are cracked open and the contents dryed into the form of a powder to make powderd eggs.

4. _____

5. _____

6. _____

7. _____

8. _____

9. _____

Eggs are good because they give us protien which helps to build and repare our body cells. Eggs are also rich in vitamens for good health, and iron, which helps to build healthy red blood sells.

10. _____

11. _____

12. _____

13. _____

One promblem is that they are also high in cholesterol so they shoud be eaten in moderation.

14. _____

15. _____

For thousands of years the egg has been a symbal of life and rebirth. At Easter, eggs are decerated and given as gifts. In China, eggs are panted bright red when a baby is born.

16. _____

17. _____

18. _____

The largast egg in the world is an ostrich egg. It would take fourty minutes to boil.

19. _____

20. _____

True or False?

1. All eggs are processed. _____

2. It is okay to eat one egg each week. _____

3. Different coloured eggs are painted when a baby is born. _____

4. Emus lay the largest eggs. _____

103

Your job is to create a healthy main meal recipe using your knowledge of the food groups. List your ingredients and the amount of each you will use. Write the procedure on how to make this meal, giving step-by-step instructions. Give your recipe an interesting name!

Name of Recipe: _____

Ingredients

_____

_____

_____

_____

_____

_____

Procedure

_____

_____

_____

_____

_____

_____

_____

_____

In this space, draw what your main meal might look like.

Pulses are the seeds of plants such as beans, lentils and peas. Many types of pulses can be found growing in different parts of the world. They can be grown in most climates. Examples of pulses include chick peas, lima beans and lentils.

Pulses are harvested by machines that extract the whole plant, separating the seeds from the pods. These seeds can be eaten fresh, but most of the time we choose to dry them first before we eat them. Once they are dried they can be stored for up to two years. Pulses are most often used in stews, dips and soups.

They are a good source of protein which help to repair our bodies. Pulses are also high in fibre which helps us to exercise our intestines. As well, they contain carbohydrate to give us energy.

Hummus, a food from Mediterranean countries, is made from a pulse called chick pea. The chick peas are cooked and mashed with lemon juice, oil and garlic. The hummus is then spread on bread or used as a dip.

Indians often eat pulses instead of meat because it is cheaper. They use pulses in dips, curries, salads and breads.

Baked beans are really navy beans, a pulse mixed with tomato sauce.

Comprehension

Answer all questions in full sentences.

1. What are pulses? _____

   _____

2. Where are pulses grown? _____

3. Are pulses good for you? How do you know? _____

   _____

4. What is hummus made from? _____

5. Why do Indians prefer pulses to meat? _____

   _____

True or False?

1. Navy beans are pulses. _____

2. Baked beans are good for you. _____

3. Most Indian people are probably poor. _____

4. Pulses can be eaten fresh. _____

5. Pulses contain lots of fats and protein. _____

An apostrophe may be used to show possession (i.e. to show that someone owns something). For example, Greg's dog;   Salvatore's arm;   Maria's holiday.

Rewrite the following sentences and insert apostrophes where necessary.

1. Jelenas diet is very healthy.

_____

2. Costas mother makes sure that he eats breakfast.

_____

3. We went to a grocers shop to buy nutritious food.

_____

4. Dianes eating habits have improved her strength.

_____

5. It is Jacques birthday today.

_____

If there is more than one owner, and the naming word ends in *s*, an apostrophe is inserted after the *s*. For example, my parents' car, the footballers' uniforms.

Rewrite the following sentences and insert apostrophes where necessary.

1. The dogs kennels need to be cleaned.

_____

2. The babies toys were all over the floor.

_____

3. Our athletes meals were carefully prepared.

_____

4. A boys school was invited to the dance.

_____

5. The girls hats looked very smart.

_____

Using Correct Punctuation

Rewrite the following sentences using correct punctuation.

1. sam believes that we should eat foods from each food group

_____

2. the best sources of protein come from foods like beans peas meat fish and eggs

_____

3. cordials cola and other fizzy drinks arent healthy because they contain sugar

_____

How to Make Sausage Sticks

The following instructions will show you how to make Sausage Sticks but there is one problem - the instructions are all mixed up! Rewrite the instructions in the correct order.

Roll each piece into the shape of a small sausage.

Eat with bread, salad or sauce.

Put mince, grated onion, chopped parsley and wheatgerm into a bowl.

Thread each sausage onto a bamboo skewer.

Mix the ingredients well.

Place the sausages under a grill.

Divide the mixture into a dozen pieces.

Grill under a medium heat and turn once.

1. _____

_____

2. _____

_____

3. _____

_____

4. _____

_____

5. _____

_____

6. _____

_____

7. _____

_____

8. _____

_____

Cloze Passage

sold	the	fish	markets	for	them	more	people

Most fish are harvested by people in fishing trawlers. They catch fish in large nets, pack _____ in ice and send them to fish _____, factories and shops. At the markets, fish is _____ to shops and to the public.

In factories, some of the _____ is cleaned, scaled, filleted and canned for _____ to eat. Some fish is also canned _____ pet foods. Japanese people catch and eat _____ fish than people in any other country in _____ world.

Read, discuss and study the word bank. Add some more theme words. Remember to LOOK, COVER, WRITE and CHECK when learning spelling.

breeze	paradise	worry	neighbour	together
company	suddenly	scrambling	breath	continue
billabong	strange	murky	danger	thought
logging	escape	destroy	wonderful	environment
moment	polluted	future	species	endangered
colony	travelled	demolish	remains	forest
_____	_____	_____	_____	_____

Activity 1

Find the meaning of the following words and then use each in a sentence.

a) endangered _____

_____

b) paradise _____

_____

c) murky _____

_____

Activity 2

Build on the given base words by adding the endings in the table.

Base word	Add s	Add ed	Add ing	Suffix
navigate	navigates	navigated	navigating	navigation
worry	_____	_____	_____	_____
demolish	_____	_____	_____	_____
pollute	_____	_____	_____	_____

Activity 3 - Word Rule

For words with the sound of "eee", write IE except after C. Practise these.

a) br___f   b) f___rce   c) sh___ld   d) th___f   e) n___ce   f) rel___f   g) s___ge

Activity 4 - FUN SPOT

Find as many theme words (there are 14) as you can from the grid.

e	n	v	i	r	o	n	m	e	n	t	h	f	e	o	t	p	b
s	f	d	e	s	t	r	o	y	b	l	s	u	y	u	h	l	r
c	o	l	o	n	y	k	m	u	r	k	y	t	t	u	o	i	e
a	e	n	d	a	n	g	e	r	e	d	m	u	r	j	u	n	a
p	h	c	o	m	p	a	n	y	l	s	t	r	a	n	g	e	t
e	d	n	t	o	g	e	t	h	e	r	a	e	s	f	h	h	h
b	i	l	l	a	b	o	n	g	v	p	o	l	l	u	t	e	d

Read the text silently then, complete activities on the following pages.

No Home

A gentle breeze blew across paradise as Kelly Koala chewed her first gum leaf of the morning. She had made sure that her children, Billy and Amy had eaten breakfast before worrying about her own meal.

She was looking forward to her morning chat to her friend, Molly, who lived in a neighbouring tree. She and Molly had been friends for years. They had raised children together and spent many happy times in each other's company.

Suddenly, there was a scrambling noise and before she could take another breath, Molly was sitting right next to her, puffing and panting.

"What's the matter, Molly? What's wrong?" asked Kelly.

"It's my baby, Kenny!" replied Molly "He's very sick. He's only had a drink of water this morning."

Kenny was clasped tightly to Molly's back. He was groaning in pain.

"We must check the billabong," declared Kelly, "There have been too many strange noises happening here lately."

They made their way down to the billabong. Their eyes widened at what they saw. There were wide tracks made by a truck or tractor and the billabong was a murky green.

"Oh no!" cried Kelly, "It's the humans. I've heard how uncaring they can be, but they have never been this close to us before. Our lives are in danger!"

Moving from tree to tree, the Koalas realised that the humans were much closer than they had thought. In fact, the humans had started cutting down trees to make way for houses that were to be built.

"We must escape to the other side of the river. Our homes are going to be destroyed! Our wonderful environment lost."

Moments later, a group of koalas came racing up to them.

"Kelly, do you mind if we share your tree?" they asked. "Our home has been knocked to the ground."

Kelly and Molly stared in horror.

"We can't stay here!" she cried, "the billabong's polluted and our homes are going to be destroyed. We must escape across the river. The future of our children and our species depends on it."

With heavy hearts, the colony of koalas travelled across the river and stared angrily at the humans on the other side who were now demolishing the remains of the forest.

"If this continues to happen, we are all doomed!" stated Kelly.

No Home

Answer all questions in full sentences.

1. What did Kelly do after her children ate breakfast? _____

_____

2. What was Kelly looking forward to? _____

_____

3. Why was Molly worried? _____

_____

4. What did Kelly and Molly notice about the billabong? _____

_____

5. Why did Kelly and Molly decide to move to the other side of the river? _____

_____

_____

6. What happened to the other koalas? _____

_____

7. What message does this story give to humans? _____

_____

_____

Vocabulary

1. Find a word from the story that means:

a) a firm hold _____   b) a waterhole _____

c) destroy   _____   d) to get away _____

e) a place of great beauty _____

True or False?

1. Molly and Kelly had known each other for a long time. _____

2. Kenny was a sick koala. _____

3. Kenny was left in a tree while Molly got help. _____

4. The billabong was a funny blue colour. _____

5. Kenny's mother is Kelly. _____

6. The humans were clearing land to build houses. _____

7. The koalas escaped to the other side of the mountain. _____

8. Humans are destroying the environment. _____

In what ways do humans damage the environment? List as many as you can below.

1. _____
2. _____
3. _____
4. _____
5. _____

Select **one** of the environmental problems you have listed and create a narrative to tell to the rest of the class. Use the planning section below to help with your talk.

Theme or main
message of the   _____
story   _____
                        _____

Orientation
Character/s   *Description of Character/s*

_____   _____

_____   _____

_____   _____

_____   _____

_____   _____

Where   _____
When   _____

Complication
Events

  • _____

  • _____

  • _____

  • _____

Resolution

  • _____

From the plan you have developed for story-telling, write the narrative in the space below.

Story Title _____

Orientation
(Who, when,
where?)

_____
_____
_____
_____
_____

Events

_____
_____
_____
_____
_____
_____
_____
_____

Complication

_____
_____
_____
_____
_____
_____
_____

Resolution

_____
_____
_____
_____
_____
_____

Circle the words that you think have been spelt incorrectly. Write the correct form of each mispelt word. There is one incorrect word for each line.

Molly and Kelly are two koalas who live on unspoylt land far
from the city. It is a place with cleen, unpolluted waterways
and fresch air.

1. _____
2. _____
3. _____

One day, Molly rushers up a tree to tell Kelly about her sick
baby, Kenny, who appeers to be in pain.

4. _____
5. _____

Kenny has drunk a small amownt of water from the nearby
billabong. When Molly and Kelly get to the billabong, thay
reelise that it has turned a murky green colour.

6. _____
7. _____
8. _____

After looking around the area, they notise that humans have
brought trucks and tracktors into the forest and are cleering
the land to make way for houses.

9. _____
10. _____
11. _____

Shortly after this, a coloney of koalas ask to share Kelly's tree
becuase their homes have been destroyed by humans.

12. _____
13. _____

It seems that the koalas are doomed unless they deside to
exscape across the river.

14. _____
15. _____

The koalas are extremely
angry and upset at
the damige that the
humans are doing to the
enviroment. However, they
must move to save there lives.

16. _____

17. _____
18. _____

Design and draw a story map of the story "No Home". Make sure that you include the main events and setting in the story. Include a key to help me to understand your map.

Story Map of   **"No Home"**
by   **R. Francis**

Key

Synonyms are words that have the same or similar meaning, e.g. ancient - old.
Find synonyms for the following.

1. steal _____   2. allow _____   3. beg _____

4. leap _____   5. crush _____   6. throw _____

Antonyms

Antonyms are words that have the opposite meaning, e.g. old - new.
Find antonyms for the following.

1. friend _____   2. stale _____   3. tidy _____

4. beginning _____   5. ignore _____   6. heavy _____

Conjunctions

The words **because, as, why, if, although** are conjunctions of cause or reason.
They are used to show when something happens. For example, You cannot wear that
shirt **because** it is dirty.
Rewrite the following pairs of sentences as one by using one of the joining words above.

1. You like the movie.   Give me one reason.

_____

2. They tried hard.   They lost the Grand Final.

_____

3. You like the roller blades.   You buy them.

_____

4. Leave the table.   You have finished your dinner.

_____

5. We were unable to play soccer.   The playing field was waterlogged.

_____

Threw or Through?

1. A cricket ball came _____ our window.
2. I quickly _____ the ball at the stumps.
3. Do you know that ghosts can walk _____ walls?
4. He _____ a paper airplane.

Hear or Here?

1. Can you _____ the beautiful music?
2. _____ are some interesting paintings.
3. _____ is the music you wanted to _____.

115

Definition

A procedure or set of instructions tells us how to do or make something.

Features

Procedures:

- use joining words of time (temporal conjunctions) such as first, next, then, when.
- use action verbs, e.g. mix, place, add.
- use adverbs, e.g. carefully, quickly, slowly.
- use the present tense.
- use common nouns, e.g. lists of ingredients: tomato, lettuce, meat.

Activities - Action Verbs

There is an action verb on each line of the instructions for making scones. Write in the spaces.

Scones

1. In a bowl, mix 2 cups of flour and salt. _____

2. Add some margarine. _____

3. Mix in a cup of milk. _____

4. Knead the mixture gently. _____

5. Pat the mixture until it is 2 cm thick. _____

6. Using a scone cutter, cut the mixture into circles. _____

7. Place circles on a baking tray. _____

8. Bake for 10 minutes in a hot oven. _____

9. Serve with jam and fresh cream. _____

Common Nouns - All the ingredients in the recipe for scones are common nouns. List them below.

1. _____   2. _____   3. _____

4. _____   5. _____   6. _____

Adverbs - There is one adverb in the scone recipe above. Write it in the space below.

_____

Follow the procedure to make a glider.

Making a Glider

Materials
- a drinking straw
- a sheet of A4 paper
- a ruler and pencils
- sticky tape
- a sheet of graph paper
- a pair of scissors

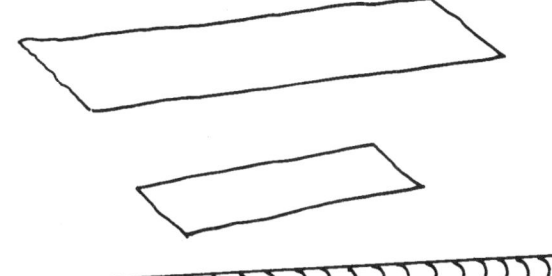

Steps
- Measure and cut two strips of paper, one 10 cm x 1.5 cm, and the other 13 cm x 2 cm.

- Make a loop with each strip of paper and allow the ends to overlap to form a pocket for the straw to fit in.
- Attach sticky tape, to both ends of each loop; one piece on the inside and one on the outside.
- Fit the straw through the pocket of each loop.
- Place the small loop at the front with the larger loop at the back and throw gently.

On a separate piece of paper, write the procedure for making a paper aeroplane. (Use diagrams)

Term 1 - Friends and Family
Spelling Worksheet (page 12)
Activity 1
Teacher to check sentences.
a) unique - different from the others
b) interact - to have an effect on each other
c) tolerate - to put up with
Activity 2
a) in-flu-ence b) e-mo-tion c) a-bi-li-ty
d) re-la-tion-ship e) spe-cial
Activity 3
a) marked, marking b) trusted, trusting
c) accepted, accepting d) respected,
    respecting   g) interacted, interacting
Activity 4
You can always trust your friend.

Talking and Listening (page 13)
Teacher to assess oral presentations.

Reading (page 14)
1. Carlos wants Matsuo to be his pen friend because he has completed a project about Japan and because he would like to learn more about the country.
2. Carlos' parents came to Australia because they couldn't find jobs and because they wanted a better life for the family.
3. We know that Carlos was an adventurous baby because he was always crawling and exploring the house.
4. Carlos liked Kindergarten because he wrote about his good report and the funny pictures that he drew.
5. Two things Carlos liked about his trip to Spain were watching bull fights and playing street soccer.

Writing - Poetry (page 15)
Teacher to check written responses.

Proofreading (page 16)
1. important 2. great 3. nappy 4. morals
5. attitudes 6. polite 7. visitors 8 period
9. arguments 10. gradually 11. sensible
12. guidance 13. because 14. responsible
15. contribution
Cloze
1. class 2. old 3. because 4. both 5. each
6. usually 7. talented 8. fight

Grammar (page 17)
Quiet or Quite?
1. quiet 2. quite 3. quite 4. quiet 5. quiet

Common and Proper Nouns
Teacher to check written responses.
Quotation Marks
1. "We will be leaving for our holidays in January," I told my friend.
2. I said to my mother, "That roller coaster was fantastic!"
3. "Would you like to swim in my pool?" asked Uncle Bruno.
4. I said to Jeanie, "Let's go to the shop and buy an ice cream."
5. "What a fantastic goal!" I yelled from the grandstand.

Reading (page 18)
1. One reason why gang members might get attacked is through walking down the wrong street.
   (Other reason: getting into arguments.)
2. Two things that may happen to people if they become violent during an argument is that someone might end up in hospital and someone may be charged with assault.
3. Children are sometimes violent when fights or disagreements occur in the playground.
4. Children who display aggressive behaviour in schools are punished.
5. The author is trying to encourage the reader to solve problems without the need for violence.

Grammar (page 19)
Action Verbs
1. walks 2. slammed 3. felt 4. swam 5. played
Relational Verbs
1. is - relational 2. dragged - action
3. sprinted - action 4. has - relational
5. are - relational
Action Verbs - walk, fish, sit, eat
Relational Verbs - have, are, have, have

Floating and Sinking
Spelling Worksheet (page 20)
Activity 1
a) predicts, predicted, predicting, prediction
b) observes, observed, observing, observation
c) discusses, discussed, discussing, discussion
d) constructs, constructed, constructing, construction
Activity 2
a) amount, measure, expand, investigate, plastic
b) equal, collect, level, water, experiment
Activity 3
a) designs b) floats c) equals d) measures e) levels
f) amounts g) collects h) alters i) observes

Activity 4
Teacher to check responses

Grammar (page 21)
By looking at an object, we can sometimes tell whether it will float or sink. A feather will probably float but something like a marble will sink. There are other objects that may float first but, if we do something to them they may sink. For example, a dry sponge may float on water while a wet sponge may sink.

Word Meanings
1. to examine closely - investigate
2. a way of doing something - procedure
3. having great meaning - important
4. to tell the future - predict
5. to write down information - record

Off, Of or From?
1. off 2. from 3. of 4. from 5. from 6. from 7. off
8. of 9. from 10. of

Reading (page 22)
1. Adult supervision is required in the making of this boat because sharp tools are being used.
2. With the sheet of cardboard you cut out your own design of a sail.
3. "Test the buoyancy of your boat..." means to check to see that the boat floats.
4. Stick the sail to the straw with Blu-Tac or plasticine.
5. **Teacher to check answers.** e.g. make the boat lighter, check for leaks, re-position the sail.

Proofreading (page 23)
1. vessels 2. return 3. surface 4. control
5. allow 6. enable 7. replaced 8. amazing
9. ability 10. engines 11. cushion 12. travelling
13. journey.

Cloze Passage
1. push 2. through 3. water 4. move 5. boat
6. speeds 7. flow 8. very

Writing (pages 24-25)
Teacher to check written responses.

Talking and Listening (page 26)
Teacher to check oral responses.

Grammar (page 27)
Antonyms
1. finish 2. smooth 3. slow 4. soft 5. near 6. old
7. fall or set 8. remember 9. hate

Prefixes - to form Antonyms
1. undo 2. disagree 3. imperfect 4. unable
5. incorrect 6. disqualify 7. indirect 8. impossible
9. unusual

Came or Come?
1. come 2. came 3. come 4. come 5. came.

Adjectives
1. strong describes the wind
2. noisy describes the crowd
3. neat describes Thao's handwriting
4. scary describes the ghost
5. untidy describes the bedroom

Australian Explorers
Spelling Worksheet (page 28)
Activity 1
Teacher to check sentences.
a) endured - to put up with for a long time
b) companion - someone going out with or travelling with another
c) descent - the act of going down

Activity 2
a) explores, explored, exploring, exploration
b) surveys, surveyed, surveying, surveyor
c) accompanies, accompanied, accompanying, accompaniment
d) travels, travelled, travelling, traveller

Activity 3
1. gate / ate 2. cover / over 3. age 4. eve
5. mount 6. company / pan / any 7. art
8. cultural 9. equip / men 10. set / settle / men
11. direct 12. end / red

Activity 4
Teacher to check answers.

Talking and Listening (page 29)
Teacher to check oral responses.

Reading (page 30)
1793 - Lieutenant John Hayes named the Derwent River.
1804 - George Harris sailed the Huon River.
1807 - Lieutenant Thomas Laycock crossed Van Diemen's Land.
1807 - Charles Grimes followed the Jordan Valley
1815-16 - James Kelly and four others circumnavigated the island in a whaleboat.
1819-20 - Henry Rice discovered good farming land when exploring the east coast.
1824 - James Hobbs and 12 convicts explored the west coast in 2 whaleboats.
1827 - Henry Hellyer explored the north-west of Tasmania.
1827 - Joseph Fossey trekked overland from Launceston to Emu Bay (now Burnie).

Proofreading (page 31)
1. first 2. Australia 3. commenced 4. experienced
5. expedition 6. appointed 7. skilled 8. detailed
9. chosen 10. organisers 11. equipped

12. Arrangements   13. Government   14. similar
Cloze Passage
1. English 2. inland 3. rivers 4. solve 5. following
6. named 7. mystery 8. explored.

Reading (page 32)
1. Five people went on this expedition.
2. The expedition was difficult because there were few waterholes and the land was barren.
3. It is believed that John Baxter was killed by Neremberein and Cootachah.
4. "Coping with the few provisions they had left" means that they had to survive on what little food and water was left.
5. Wylie stayed in Albany in the west and became a local celebrity.

Grammar (page 33)
Interesting Sentences - Teacher to check sentences.
Full Stops and Capital Letters
1. John Septimus Roe explored the south coast of Western Australia.
2. Ludwig Leichhardt arrived in Sydney and wanted to explore Central Australia.
3. Charles Sturt was always friendly towards Aboriginal people.
4. William Hovell was a farmer and ex-sea captain.
5. Hamilton Hume spent his childhood exploring the area around Berrima.
Antonyms
1. awake 2. pass / succeed 3. slow 4. soft/quiet
5. before 6. attack 7. go 8. shrink
Very or Real?
1. very 2. very 3. real

Grammar (page 34)
Kinds of Sentences
1. Statement 2. Question 3. Command
4. Statement 5. Question
Commas
1. Ludwig Leichhardt was interested in Australia's rocks, plants and animals.
2. Edward John Eyre found Lakes Torrens, Eyre, Blanche, Calabonna and Frome.
3. Hamilton Hume travelled with John Oxley, James Meehan and Charles Throsby.
4. George Evans was an artist, teacher, writer, bushman, bookseller and explorer.
5. A way through the mountains was found by Blaxland, Lawson and Wentworth.
One Word for Several
1. unable to be passed - impassable
2. able to do a variety of things - versatile
3. a long period of dry weather - drought
4. a journey made for a special purpose - expedition
5. one who studies plants - botanist

Writing - Recount (page 35)
Teacher to check written responses.

Narrative - Tutorial
Past Tense (page 36)
1. She travelled to Melbourne to buy new tools.
2. Maurice dove spectacularly to save the shot.
3. The car flew around the corner at great speed.
4. He stumbled and fell as he tried to escape.
5. Jane sacked the worker because he was dishonest.
Action Verbs - Teacher to check written responses.
Examples of Narratives
Cinderella (page 37)
Characters
Cinderella, 2 Ugly stepsisters, Stepmother, Fairy Godmother, Prince.
What: Cinderella is poorly treated by her stepsisters and stepmother. A Ball is announced but Cinderella is not allowed to attend.
When: At night.
Where: In town.
Events
• A Fairy Godmother appears to Cinderella.
• Fairy Godmother helps Cinderella go to the Ball.
• Cinderella attends and captures the heart of the Prince.
• The clock strikes twelve and Cinderella must leave. Cinderella loses one of her glass slippers as she leaves.
Complications
• Prince does not know who this mystery lady is.
• Prince picks up glass slipper, determined to find its owner.
Resolution
• The glass slipper fits Cinderella who is overjoyed.
• The Ugly stepsisters and the Stepmother are horrified.
• Cinderella marries and lives happily with her Prince.
Snow White
Orientation - Characters
Snow White, Wicked Queen, Prince, Seven Drawrfs, Woodcutter
What: Wicked Queen is jealous of Snow White's beauty. She commands a huntsman to kill her.
When: One morning
Where: In the forest
Events:
• Huntsman takes pity on Snow White.
• Huntsman leaves Snow White in forest.
• Snow White finds house belonging to Seven Dwarfs.
• Seven Dwarfs welome Snow White.

Complications
- Wicked queen consults mirror and finds out that Snow White is still alive.
- Wicked Queen plots to kill Snow White
- Wicked Queen sells Snow White a poisoned apple
- Snow White bites into the apple and falls unconscious
- Seven Dwarfs, thinking Snow White is dead, carry her in a glass coffin to be buried.

Resolution:
- A Prince comes riding along and sees the glass coffin
- Prince falls in love with Snow White.
- As coffin is dropped, the piece of poisoned apple falls out of Snow White's mouth and she awakens.
- Snow White and Prince get married
- Wicked Queen finds out about Snow White and smashes the mirror. Parts of the shattered glass kill the Wicked queen.

Term 2 - The Wheelchair
Spelling Worksheet (page 40)
Activity 1
One-syllable words - sigh, thought, stroke, through, blur
Two-syllable words - wheelchair, collapse, although, tremble, question, allowed, answer, relief, doctor, moment, anger, tumbling
Three-syllable words - remember, hospital, motionless, tomorrow, overheard, yesterday, frustration, condition, wonderful
Four-syllable words - helicopter, paraplegic, competition, quadriplegic

Activity 2
1. allowed 2. although 3. anger 4. answer 5. blur
6. collapse 7. competition 8. condition 9. doctor
10. frustration 11. helicopter 12. hospital
13. moment 14. motionless 15. overheard
16. paraplegic 17. quadriplegic 18. question
19. relief 20. remember 21. sigh 22. stroke
23. thought 24. through 25. tomorrow 26. tremble
27. tumbling 28. wheelchair 29. wonderful
30. yesterday

Activity 3
a) lovelier, loveliest   b) lonelier, loneliest
c) merrier, merriest   d) wearier, weariest
e) happier, happiest   f) healthier, healthiest

Activity 4 - Teacher to check.

Reading - The Wheelchair (page 41)
No answers required.

Reading - Comprehension (page 42)
1. Vince was in hospital because he felt a crack in his neck when he was in a scrum.

2. Vince was transported to hospital by helicopter.
3. Vince played Rugby League football.
4. Vince was frightened by what had happened. The two words in the passage that show how he felt are frustration and anger.
5. The bad news that the doctor gave Vince was that he would never play football again.
6. The good news that the doctor gave Vince was that he would be able to walk again.
7. Vince was afraid to sleep because he feared that he might not wake up.

Vocabulary
1 a) collapse   b) montionless   c) trembling
  d) allowed   e) frustration

True or False
1. False   2. True   3. False   4. False
5. False   6. False   7. True   8. True

Proofreading (page 43)
1. electricity 2. spine 3. unable 4. whistle 5. trying
6. facing 7. recognised 8. They 9. could 10. certain
11. terrible 12. minutes 13. heard 14. brace
15. stretcher 16. remembered 17. waking
18. hospital 19. tone 20. scared.

Writing - Discussion (pages 44-45)
Teacher to check written responses.

Reading (page 46)
Story Setting
Teacher to check written responses.

Grammar (page 47)
Punctuation
"No!" yelled Vince's mother.
She looked over towards Vince and collapsed into a chair.
"This can't be happening," Bruno said. He held his head in his hands.

Adverbs
1. properly 2. slowly 3. clumsily 4. quickly
5. hopefully

Synonyms (Sample Answers)
a) hard b) right c) fast d) small e) fix f) carry

Space
Spelling Worksheet (page 48)
Activity 1
One-syllable words - Earth, Mars.
Two-syllable words - Pluto, shuttle, solar, system, Saturn, Neptune, comet, eclipse, Venus, orbit, planet
Three-syllable words - asteroid, Mercury, meteor, alien, astronaut, Uranus, galaxy, satellite, Jupiter, milky way, universe, telescope, gravity
Four-syllable words - constellation, astronomy, intelligence, observatory

Activity 2
1. sat, at, turn, urn   2. plan, net, plane, lane, an
3. sat, at, ate, tell, lit, it   4. cope, cop, scope

Activity 3
1. angrily 2. noisily 3. readily 4. steadily 5. speedily
6. wearily 7. warily 8. hastily 9. merrily

Activity 4
1. Pluto 2. shuttle 3. orbit 4. meteor 5. eclipse
6. gravity 7. telescope 8. astronaut 9. universe
10. intelligence 11. comet 12. asteroid.

Talking and Listening (page 49)
Group Discussion - Teacher to check oral
    responses.

Grammar (page 50)
Joining Words
1. I raced over to James who told me about the
    car accident.
2. This is the new mystery novel that I borrowed
    from the Library.
3. There is the horse that won the Melbourne Cup.
4. I am the salesman who works in the Menswear
    Department.
5. Melina is a girl who won a prize in the colouring-
    in competition.

Writing (pages 50-51)
Narrative - Teacher to check written responses.

Reading (page 52)
Teacher to check written responses.

Proofreading (page 53)
1. claimed 2. surface 3. crater 4. according
5. consultant 6. While 7. co-pilot 8. incident
9. Control 10. broadcasts 11. believed 12. signals
13. were 14. American 15. strange 16. cylinder
17. they 18. collision 19. mysteriously.

Grammar (page 54)
A man, Gary Storey, who was interested in UFOs,
claims to have exchanged messages with an
unidentified object. He set up a telescope on July
27, 1967 to observe the moon, but a bright light
attracted his attention.

Storey's brother-in-law flashed a torch at the
object three times and the object responded by
flashing its light the same number of times. After
continuing to flash its lights, the object vanished
behind some trees.
Took or Taken?
1. taken 2. took 3. took 4. taken 5. taken
Spoke or Spoken?
1. spoken 2. spoke 3. spoke 4. spoke 5. spoken

Reading (page 55)
1. Mars is 228 million kilometres from the Sun.
2. Mars is called the red planet because of the iron
    oxide or rust in its soil.
3. The surface of Mars is desert with ice caps at
    either end. It is dusty and you may find boulders,
    extinct volcanos giant canyons and dried up river
    beds.
4. Carbon dioxide is mainly found in Mars'
    atmosphere.
5. There may be life on Mars. We know this because
    a Martian meteorite showed signs of ancient life.
True or False?
1. True 2. False 3. False 4. True

Newspapers
Spelling Worksheet (page 56)
Activity 1
a) amuse b) issue c) headlines d) interview
e) national
Activity 2
a) journal, our, urn, list   b) new, news, paper, ape
c) photo, hot, graph, rap d) edit, editor, it, or,
e) car, cart, art, to, too
Activity 3
a) measuring   b) rescuing   c) scribbling
d) describing   e) amusing   f) exciting
g) escaping   h) bathing
i) pleasing.
Activity 4 - Teacher to check.

Reading (page 57)
1. The purpose of an editorial is to debate issues in
    the community.
2. The Chief Editor writes the editorial.
3. An editor should be careful about the topics
    written about because some topics may be very
    sensitive.
4. An editor usually writes about current news issues
    that are of interest to the community.
5. An editorial can influence readers to form an
    opinion.
True or False?
1. False 2. True 3. False 4. True 5. True

Talking and Listening (page 58)
Teacher to check.

Writing (page 59)
Editorial - teacher to check.

Grammar (page 60)
Using Quotation Marks
1. A passing motorist said,"The car just rammed
    straight into the pole."

2. The injured cricketer stated," I expect to be back in training next season."
3. "The blaze took control very quickly," said the fireman.
4. The Prime Minister declared," We will do all we can to help the needy."
5. "What do you think caused the accident?" asked the reporter.

Using Better Words (Sample Answers)
1. I need to purchase a new jumper.
2. I must admit I don't understand what you are saying.   3. We have to leave soon.
4. Could you please buy me a newspaper ?
5. She receives a prize for winning the competition.

Past or Passed?
1. passed 2. past 3. passed 4. passed 5. past

Reading (page 61)
News Report
1. The Australian team appears most likely to win the Test.
2. This team is most likely to win the Test because the West Indies only scored 211 runs.
3. Shane Warne is a spin bowler.
4. What made Warne's performance magnificent is the fact that he'd recently had an operation on his spinning finger.
5. Warne feels that his injured finger is as good as it has ever been.

True or False?
1. False 2. True 3. False 4. True 5. True

Proofreading (page 62)
1. critically 2. accidents 3. Hospital 4. damage
5. collapsed 6. steep 7. raised 8. Emergency
9. medical 10. breathing 11. assisting 12. sprained
13. attended.

Cloze Passage
1. burnt 2. last 3. through 4. shortly 5. residents
6 one 7. suffering 8. treated

Grammar (page 63)
Alliteration - Teacher to check responses.
Action Verbs
1. spilled 2. crashed 3. escaped 4. rescued 5. lit
Past Tense
1. The batsman scored a magnificent century.
2. The Prime Minister introduced a law.
3. The child played games on a computer.
4. The weary man mowed the lawn.
5. A lonely man found a friend.

Argument / Exposition - Tutorial
Conjunctions/Joining Words
1. The road was blocked so we had to make a detour.

2. Because the roof had a leak, the carpet was soaking wet.
3. I felt ill so I decided to go to bed.
4. Children should exercise regularly because some children are overweight.
5. We should care for our waterways as marine life is dying.

Strong Emotive Words
We should all have heroes. I firmly believe they give us a role model to look up to. Kieren Perkins for example is an excellent example.
It is certain that hard work made him achieve high standards. (example)

Term 3 - Narrative - The Mild Colonial Boy
Spelling Worksheet (page 66)
Activity 1
a) devastated b) handkerchief c) capture
d) protect · e) secretary
Activity 2
b) escape - escapes, escaped, escaping, escapee
c) terrify - terrifies, terrified, terrifying, terrific
d) behave - behaves, behaved, behaving, behaviour
e) deliver, delivers, delivered, delivering, delivery
Activity 3
a) billow - to swirl or rise
b) casual - without thinking
c) vow - a solemn promise
Activity 4
Teacher to check responses.

Reading (page 67)
No answers required.

Proofreading (page 68)
1. story 2. parents 3. because 4. their 5. becoming
6. speaks 7. driver 8. adventures 9. manager
10. surprised 11. guard 12. troopers 13. court
14. angry 15. twenty 16. die 17. escape 18. officer
19. keys   20. quickly 21. creeps 22. heard.

Writing - News Report (page 69)
Teacher to check written response.

Grammar (page 70)
Using Speech Marks
1. Bill said, "I'm very lonely because I have no family and no friends."
2. "How much money would you like?" asked Mr Molloy.

3. "The Mild Colonial Boy stole my money!"gasped Mr Molloy.
4. "Stand and deliver!" called out the Mild Colonial Boy.
5. "Please come in," replied Mrs Grimble.

Contractions
1. We'll 2. Who's 3. You're 4. don't 5. didn't
Nouns, Verbs, Adjectives.
Teacher to check answers.

Talking and Listening (page 71)
Teacher to check.

Reading - Wanted Poster (page 72)
Teacher to check.

Grammar (page 73)
Instead of 'said'
Teacher to check answers.
Adverbs
1. fiercely 2. carefully 3. suspiciously 4. sheepishly
5. ferociously
Homonyms
"Be quiet, my dear bushranger," said Mr Molloy. Although he was happy to see, The Mild Colonial Boy in prison, Mr Molloy wanted him taken to court straight away. There, was not a moment to lose. "I'm glad we have caught, you," cried Mr Molloy, "I hope you will be here for ninety-nine years." "Now there are plenty of jobs for you to do," replied Mr Molloy.

Bushrangers

Spelling Worksheet (page 74)
Activity 1
a) accomplice - someone who shares in a crime
b) notorious - well-known for something bad
c) surround - to go around completely
Teacher to check sentences.
Activity 2
a) murders, murdered, murdering, murderer
b) attacks, attacked, attacking, attacker
c) surrounds, surrounded, surrounding, -
d) hangs, hanged, hanging, hanger
Activity 3
gold - old   robbed - rob, bed
wanted - want, an, ant   hotel - hot
accomplice - ice   trooper - troop
infamous - in, famous, us   outlaw - out, law
capture - cap
bushranger - bush, range, ranger, anger, an
ballad - ball, lad   surround - round
Activity 4
Teacher to check responses.

Grammar (page 75)
Using the Correct Word
1. did 2. saw 3. were 4. rode 5. gave
Synonyms
1. right 2. hop 3. run 4. hand 5. hid

Antonyms
1. innocent - guilty   2. huge - tiny
3. straight - crooked   4. loose - tight
5. rough - smooth
Adjectives
Teacher to check answers
Adverbs - Sample Answers only
1. loudly 2. frantically 3. merrily 4. sweetly
5. carefully

Writing (pages 76-77)
Teacher to check written responses.

Reading (pages 78-79)
1. Martin Cash was sent to NSW because he committed burglary.
2. Cash left the NSW colony to settle in Campbelltown, Tasmania because he was accused of stealing cattle.
3. Cash was sentenced to seven year's hard labour for stealing farm produce and eggs.
4. Cash had to serve two extra years on top of his sentence because he escaped from gaol.
5. Cash met the two bushrangers from NSW in gaol at Port Arthur, near Hobart.
6. Cash, Jones and Kavanagh escaped from prison by swimming naked across an inlet to avoid the guards and dogs.
7. Mrs Cash was arrested because she tried to sell stolen goods.
8. Cash wanted to take revenge on Mrs Cash and Thomas Pratt because Mrs Cash abandoned him to live with Thomas Pratt.

Timeline
1809 - Martin cash born in County Wexford, Ireland.
1828 - Sent to NSW for seven years for burglary.
1837 - Cash fled NSW for Campbelltown, Tasmania.
1837 - 1854
• Sentenced to 7 years' hard labour at Port Arthur for stealing farm produce and eggs.
• Escaped but recaptured and given 2 more years to serve.
• Escaped from Port Arthur with George Jones and Lawrence Kavanagh.
• Committed many robberies and built a fort of logs and earth for protection.

• Mrs Cash arrested for attempting to sell stolen goods.
• Cash threatened the Governor with flogging unless Mrs Cash was set free.
• Mrs Cash released but abandoned Cash to live with Thomas Pratt.
• Police ambush Cash, Jones and Kavanagh in Hobart.

- Jones sentenced to death, Cash and Kavanagh sent to Norfolk Island for life.

1854 - Cash returns to Tasmania with a convict woman servant as his wife, having been given a ticket of leave. He was a caretaker of Government Gardens.

1878 - Cash died.

Proofreading (page 80)
1. Wales 2. station 3. everyone 4. robbed
5. mortgage 6. owe.
1. desperately 2. blood 3. morning 4. after
5. escaped.

Cloze Passage
1. because 2. people 3. occasion 4. life 5. house
6. bushranger 7. who 8. instead 9. Bathurst
10. husband's.

Grammar (page 81)
Using Capital Letters
1. John Donahoe was born in Dublin in 1806.
2. Captain Melville spent Christmas in Geelong.
3. Frank Gardiner was sent to the prison on Cockatoo Island.
4. The Kelly Gang were camped at Stringybark Creek.
5. John Caesar arrived in New South Wales in March 1789.

Collective Nouns
1. army 2. cluster 3. litter 4. board 5. school 6. choir
7. fleet 8. swarm

The Comma
1. Michael Howe, a sailor, became a highwayman.
2. Ned Kelly, a hero to many, was executed in 1880.
3. Johnny Dunn, a former jockey, joined Ben Hall's gang.
4. Morgan, a cold blooded killer, was shot by Paddy Quinlan.

Endangered Animals

Spelling Worksheet (page 82)
Activity 1
a) introduces, introduced, introducing, introduction
b) conserves, conserved, conserving, conservation
c) protects, protected, protecting, protection
d) survives, survived, surviving, survival

Activity 2
1. occurred, occurring
2. slipper, slipped, slipping
3. planner, planned, planning

Activity 3
clear - ear forest - for, rest capture - cap
breed - reed herbivore - herb rare - are
threat - eat, at habitat - habit, at
mountain - mount, in compete - pet
pesticide - pest swamp - swam, am

Activity 4
Teacher to check responses.

Reading (page 83)
Description - Reddish brown colour with markings across the rump, black stripe across each side of its eyes.
Food - termites and ants.
Habitat - in low scrub and hollow logs of eucalypt forests in a small part of Western Australia.
Babies - Attach themselves to teats and cling to the fur of mother's belly. Protects young by digging a burrow with a nest at the end.
Why this animal is endangered - Forests are being cleared, threatened by predators, e.g. fox.

Grammar (page 84)
Using Pronouns
Baw Baw Frogs live high on Mt Baw Baw in Victoria. (They, It) are becoming endangered because Mt Baw Baw has been developed as a ski resort. (His, Their) habitat has been destroyed.
(They, It) tend to live near water under rocks and logs. (You, I) may find small warts on (him, them).

Conjunctions
1. There were many woodhens because they had no natural predators.
2. Northern hairy-nosed wombats eat grasses and other vegetation.
3. Numbats sleep at night and are awake by day.
4. Leadbeater's possum was believed to be extinct but they were re-discovered in 1961.
5. Ghost bats are endangered because mining has destroyed their habitat.

Antonyms and Synonyms
quiet - loud - still quick - slow - fast
coarse - smooth - rough help - helpless - assist
easy - difficult - simple false - true - untrue

Writing (page 85)
Teacher to check written response.

Proofreading (page 86)
1. grey 2. Australia 3. nocturnal 4. night 5. lizards
6. before 7. killing 8. mining 9. destroy

Comprehension
1. The thing that is unique about this type of bat is that it's the only carnivorous bat in Australia.
2. You will find Ghost bats in the north of Australia.
3. The Ghost bat is beginning to die out because mining operations are destroying its habitat.
4. The sentence that proves that Ghost bats are carnivorous is, "They eat small animals such as frogs, birds, lizards and mice".
5. The Ghost bats' habitat is in caves or mines in the north of Australia.

True or False?
1. False 2. False 3. True 4. False 5. False

Grammar (page 87)
Using Commas
1. The Nabarlek, a kind of wallaby, usually grazes at night.
2. The Platypus, a marsupial, sleeps for most of the day.
3. Our favourite animal, the Koala, eats only eucalyptus leaves.
4. A nocturnal animal, the Kowari, hunts large insects and mice.
5. Like the Cuscus, the Striped possum lives alone.

Punctuation
Like all cockatoos, pink cockatoos have strong beaks which they use to crack seeds and nuts. They feed on the seeds of grasses and the fruits of trees like wattles, cypress pines and she-oaks. You will find them in the dry centre of Australia although they have been found near the coast in Victoria and South Australia.

Went or Gone?
1. gone 2. went 3. gone 4. went

Talking and Listening (page 88)
Teacher to check oral responses.

Writing - Discussion (page 89)
Teacher to check written responses.

Information Report - Tutorial
Present Tense
1. There <u>are</u> over 3 000 species of spiders.
2. The spider's silk <u>is</u> strong and elastic.
3. Spiders <u>produce</u> silk from glands in the abdomen.
4. A spider <u>crushes</u> the hard parts of its victims body.
5. Some spiders <u>perform</u> courtship dances.

Relational Verbs
1. has 2. are 3. are 4. have 5. belong to 6. have

Term 4 - The Human Body
Spelling Worksheet (page 92)
Activity 1
1. cardiac - having to do with the heart.
2. cartilage - firm, elastic substance forming part of the bone structure
3. retina - coating on the back of the eyeball which picks up the image of what you see

Activity 2
1. collar, bone, one, on 2. ear, hear, art
3. cart, art, age. 4. ear, drum, rum

Activity 3
a) believes   b) lives   c) wives   d) thieves
e) halves f) shelves g) grieves h) wolves   i) calves

Activity 4
CAST - CART - CARD - CORD - WORD
MINT - MINE - MITE - MATE - DATE

Grammar (page 93)
Conjunctions
1. I will do the dishes <u>while</u> you dry the dishes.
2. Go soon, <u>before</u> the shops close.
3. He will give me the money <u>when</u> I see him tomorrow.
4. You should brush your teeth <u>before</u> you go to school.
5. You may not have dessert <u>until</u> you finish your dinner.

Using Correct Punctuation
The human body is made up of a number of systems. It is an amazing machine. Some of the systems include the circulatory, the nervous and the skeletal systems.
We should make sure that we look after our bodies. This will keep us healthy.

Synonyms and Antonyms
miserable - unhappy - happy
defeat - beat - victory
high - tall - low
complete - finish - incomplete
leave - go - arrive

Reading (page 94)
1. Blood is made up of plasma, red blood cells, platelets and white blood cells.
2. Plasma takes proteins, chemicals, food and wastes around the body.
3. The purpose of white blood cells is to fight and destroy bacteria.
4. The different types of blood vessels are arteries, veins and capillaries.
5. If you were given a blood transfusion from the wrong group, severe reactions may occur or even death.

True or False?
1. True 2. False 3. True 4. False

Proofreading (page 95)
1. consists 2. enables 3. important 4. heart 5. muscles
6. where 7. shoulders 8. because 9. direction 10. toes
11. special 12. column 13. brittle 14. their
15. fractured 16. There 17. injury 18. Instead 19. medical.

True or False?
1. False 2. True 3. True 4. False 5. True

Grammar (page 96)
Apostrophes to Shorten Words
1. you're 2. wasn't 3. I've 4. we'll 5. I'd 6. she's 7. can't

8. they're 9. here's

1. could not 2. have not 3. she will 4. must not
5. you are 6. he would

Good or Well?

1. well 2. well 3. good 4. good 5. well

Wrote or Written?

1. written 2. wrote 3. written 4. wrote 5. written

There, They're or Their?

1. They're 2. their 3. There 4. there 5. They're, their

Reading (page 97)

1. Before the food can be used for growth and energy it must be digested.
2. Our saliva helps us to digest food by mixing with the chewed food, softening it and making it easier to swallow.
3. Before it gets to the stomach, food passes through the oesophagus.
4. In the stomach the food is churned and mixed with digestive juices and acid.
5. The intestines help in the digestive system by allowing food to be absorbed by the body and by moving wastes through.

True or False?

1. True 2. True 3. True 4. False 5. False

Writing - Science Experiment (pages 98-99)
Teacher to check written responses.

Food and Nutrition

Spelling Worksheet (page 100)
Activity 1

a) the wish for food and drink - appetite
b) to break down in your stomach and intestines - digest
c) the state of being lazy - lethargic
d) to give out a salty liquid through the skin - sweat
e) soft silver-white metal found in teeth and bones - calcium
f) the part of food that can't be digested - fibre

Activity 2

1. appetite 2. balance 3. benefit 4. breakfast
5. calcium 6. carbohydrate 7. dairy 8. digest
9. energy 10. fibre 11. fluid 12. growth 13. health
14. hunger 15. important 16. ingredient
17. lethargic 18. minerals 19. nutrition 20. protein
21. restless 22. strength 23. substance 24. sugar
25. survive 26. sweat 27. thirst
28. vegetables 29. vitamins 30. weight

Activity 3

a) silos b) radios c) studios d) zeros e) banjos
f) sopranos g) solos h) rodeos i) merinos

Activity 4
Teacher to check.

Talking and Listening (page 101)
Teacher to check oral responses.

Grammar (page 102)
Conjunctions

1. I like to drink milk <u>and</u> fruit juice.
2. Coffee <u>and</u> cola contain a dangerous drug called caffeine.
3. A little salt is okay <u>but</u> too much salt increases your blood pressure.
4. We tried to improve his diet <u>but</u> he would not follow the diet.
5. Milk <u>and</u> cheese contain calcium for strong bones and teeth.

Prefixes

1. rearrange 2. recount 3. refresh 4. recycle
5. replay 6. regain 7. recreate 8. recover 9. reheat

1. prepare - to make or get ready
2. prelude - something that comes before
3. predict - tell what is going to happen in the future
4. precede - to go before
5. precaution - something done in advance to prevent problems

Teacher to check sentences

Proofreading (page 103)

1. eaten 2. raised 3. climate 4. batteries 5. laid
6. taken 7. cartons 8. dried 9. powdered
10. protein 11. repair 12. vitamins 13. cells
14. problem 15. should 16. symbol
17. decorated 18. painted 19. largest 20. forty.

True or False?

1. False 2. True 3. False 4. False

Writing (page 104)
Teacher to check written responses.

Reading (page 105)

1. Pulses are the seeds of plants like beans, peas and lentils.
2. Pulses are grown in most climates in different parts of the world.
3. Pulses are good for you because the protein in them helps to repair our bodies. Pulses exercise our intestines because they are high in fibre and they contain carbohydrates, which give us energy.
4. Hummus is made from chick peas.
5. Indians prefer pulses to meat because it's cheaper.

True or False?

1. True 2. True 3. True 4. True 5. False

Grammar (page 106)
Apostrophe of Possession

1. Jelena's diet is very healthy.

2. Costa's mother makes sure that he eats breakfast.
3. We went to a grocer's shop to buy nutritious food.
4. Diane's eating habits have improved her strength.
5. It is Jacques' birthday today.
1. The dogs' kennels need to be cleaned.
2. The babies' toys were all over the floor.
3. Our athletes' meals were carefully prepared.
4. A boys' school was invited to the dance.
5. The girls' hats looked very smart.

Using Correct Punctuation

1. Sam believes that we should eat foods from each food group.
2. The best sources of protein come from foods like beans, peas, meat, fish and eggs.
3. Cordials, cola and other fizzy drinks aren't healthy because they contain sugar.

Reading (page 107)

• Put mince, grated onion, chopped parsley and wheatgerm into a bowl.
• Mix the ingredients well.
• Divide the mixture into a dozen pieces.
• Roll each piece into the shape of a small sausage.
• Thread each sausage onto a bamboo skewer.
• Place the sausages under a grill.
• Grill under a medium heat and turn once.
• Eat with bread, salad or sauce.

Cloze Passage

1. them 2. markets 3. sold 4. fish 5. people 6. for
7. more 8. the

No Home

Spelling Worksheet (page 108)

Activity 1
a) endangered - in danger or at risk
b) paradise - a place of great beauty
c) murky - dark and gloomy

Activity 2
a) worries, worried, worrying, worrier
b) demolishes, demolished, demolishing, demolition
c) pollutes, polluted, polluting, pollution

Activity 3
a) brief b) fierce c) shield d) thief e) niece
f) relief g) siege

Activity 4
Teacher to check.

Reading (page 109)

No answers required.

Reading - Comprehension (page 110)

1. After her children ate breakfast, Kelly chewed some gum leaves.
2. Kelly was looking forward to her morning chat with Molly.
3. Molly was worried because her baby, Kenny, was sick.

4. Kelly and Molly noticed that the billabong was a murky green colour.
5. Kelly and Molly decided to move to the other side of the river because they feared that their homes would be destroyed and that they might die.
6. The other koalas had their trees knocked down.
7. The message that this story gives to humans is to protect our environment or we will destroy ourselves.

Vocabulary

1. a) clasping b) billabong c) demolishing
   d) escape e) paradise

True or False?

1. True 2. True 3. False 4. False 5. False 6. True
7. False 8. True

Talking and Listening (page 111)

Teacher to check oral responses.

Writing (page 112)

Teacher to check written responses.

Proofreading (page 113)

1. unspoilt 2. clean 3. fresh 4. rushes 5. appears
6. amount 7. they 8. realise 9. notice 10. tractors
11. clearing 12. colony 13. because 14. decide
15. escape 16. damage 17. environment 18. their

Reading - Story Map (page114)

Teacher to check work.

Grammar (page 115)

Synonyms
1. take 2. permit 3. plead 4. jump 5. break 6. fling(examples)

Antonyms
1. enemy 2. fresh 3. untidy 4. end 5. notice 6. light.

Conjunctions
1. Give me one reason why you like the movie.
2. Although they tried hard, they lost the Grand Final.
3. If you like the roller blades, buy them.
4. If you have finished your dinner leave the table.
5. We were unable to play soccer because the playing field was waterlogged.

Threw or Through?
1. through 2. threw 3. through 4. threw

Hear or Here?
1. hear 2. Here 3. Here, hear

Tutorial - Text Type - Procedure

Action Verbs
1. mix 2. add 3. mix 4. knead 5. pat 6. cut 7. place
8. bake 9. serve.

Common Nouns
1. flour 2. salt 3. margarine 4. milk 5. jam 6. cream

Adverbs
1. gently